12/08

P9-AQO-151

In the Garden with Jane Austen

Donated by

Friends of

**The Woodbridge
Library**

© DEMCO, INC. 1990 PRINTED IN U.S.A.

IN THE
Garden WITH
Jane Austen

Kim Wilson

JONES BOOKS
Madison, Wisconsin

Copyright © Kim Wilson 2008
All rights reserved

Jones Books
309 N. Hillside Terrace
Madison, Wisconsin 53705
jonesbooks.com

First edition, first printing

Notes on the Text: Jane Austen's original, occasionally idiosyncratic spelling (for example, she often substituted "ei" for "ie"), capitalization, and punctuation appear unchanged in this book. Some abbreviations have been expanded for clarity.

Photo credits: pp. 58-59 by kind permission of Bath Tourism Plus; cover photo, pp. 18-19, 25 © by kind permission of Blenheim Palace and Jarrolds Publishing; pp. viii, x, 2 5, 9, 15, 16, 23, 32, 43, 46, 48, 60, 92, 93, 94, 96 top, inside cover photo by Ellen Byler; p. 26 © Chatsworth House Trust, photo by Gary Rogers; pp. 35, 37 photos kindly supplied by Dudley Council; p. 44 by kind permission of Lady Fitzwalter; p. 98 garden plan by kind permission of Gilbert White's House; p. 95 garden plan by Patricia Hopkins, Jane Austen's House Museum; pp. vi, 6 by David Quick; pp. 40, 100 bottom by kind permission of Stoneleigh Abbey; p. 102 garden plan by kind permission of the Kennard Hotel; p. 57 by kind permission of The Royal Crescent Hotel; pp. xii, 1, 11, 13, 14, 17, 20, 29, 39, 42, 47, 50-51, 52, 54, 55, 61, 62, 64, 67, 70, 72-73, 74, 76, 79, 80, 83, 85, 87, 88-89, 90, 96 bottom, 97, 99, 100 top, 101, 103 by Kim Wilson.

Library of Congress Cataloging-in-Publication Data

Wilson, Kim, 1959-
In the garden with Jane Austen / Kim Wilson. — 1st ed.
    p. cm.
Includes bibliographical references and index.
ISBN 978-0-9790475-1-0 (alk. paper)
1. Austen, Jane, 1775-1817 2. Gardens, English. 3. Plants, Ornamental. I. Title.
SB457.6.W554 2008
712.0942'09034—dc22
                    2008022663

Printed in China

To Charlie

Rosa gallica versicolor "Rosa Mundi" grows in the Rose Garden at Chawton Cottage, Jane Austen's House Museum.

Contents

Foxgloves at Chawton Cottage, Jane Austen's House Museum

Foreword

In the garden with Jane Austen . . . how wonderful that would be to see the very plants that she would have known, looked at, treasured and brushed past as she ventured out into garden or field.

If you have never read any of Jane Austen's stories, you will find here amongst these pages many extracts and quotes from her books and letters, as well as information about garden design and plans.

Many plants growing within gardens of the time were wildflowers, or even weeds by today's standards. Most country cottage gardens would have been a complete mix of wildflowers, cultivated flowers, fruit and vegetable plants. The shrubbery was quite an important part of the garden, providing the inhabitants or visitors with seclusion and privacy. Now, 200 years later, quantities of saved seeds have provided the garden at Chawton Cottage with a wonderful array of flowers. But it still must be said that, as in Jane Austen's day, the mignonette seed continues not to germinate well.

Celia Simpson
Head Gardener, Jane Austen's House

Columbines in the garden at Chawton Cottage, Jane Austen's House Museum

Acknowledgments

I must first thank the owners, gardeners, managers, and guides of the garden sites I visited for their kind assistance and warm hospitality, in particular Celia Simpson, Tom Carpenter, and Pat Hopkins of Jane Austen's House Museum; Sara Pengelly of Chawton House Library; Mr. and Mrs. John Sunley, Greg Ellis, and Jenny Cooper of Godmersham Park; David Standing of Gilbert White's House; Anthea Busk of Houghton Lodge; Jean and Robert Stephens of Stubbs Farm; Mary and Giovanni Baiano of the Kennard Hotel in Bath; John Bennett of the Royal Crescent Hotel in Bath; Martin James and Eileen Mogridge of Stoneleigh Abbey; Kate and Jack Wilson in Chawton; and Joyce Bown in Steventon. I am also very grateful for the gracious assistance of the others who helped me in the preparation of the book: Ann Channon, Louise West, Janet Johnstone, Pat Kitching, and the staff of Jane Austen's House Museum; Susie Grandfield, Corrinne Saint, and Heather Shearer of Chawton House Library; Donald Ramsay of Basildon Park; Eleanor Murphy of the Bath Preservation Trust; Lucy Weaver of Bath Tourism Plus; Hannah Payne of Blenheim Palace; Kay Rotchford of Chatsworth House; Jill Palmer of Dorney Court; Flair Kitching of Gilbert White's House; Lady Fitzwalter and Francis Plumptre of Goodnestone Park; Carrie Goodhew and Lynn Silvester of Groombridge Place; Jorge De Matos Ferreira of Ham House; David Baldock, Sally Collins, and Terry Old of the Jane Austen Centre in Bath; Sue Grant of Loseley Park; Philip Burt of Lyme Park; Sarah Baker of Montacute House; Sasha Jackson of Newby Hall; Glenn Humphreys of the Parks Department in Bath; Sharon Love of the Royal Crescent Hotel in Bath; Martin Ellis and Amanda Wilson of the Royal Pavilion in Brighton; Paula Cornwell, Jeannette Kerr, Derek Robinson, and Shahab Seyfollahi of Stoneleigh Abbey; Ewan Chapman and Jo Whitehouse of The Leasowes; Anne Arthur and Victoria Owen of The Old Rectory; Ben Boyle of The Vyne; Christine Davis; Richard Knight; David Quick; and Dr. C.J. Rushforth. Thanks go also to my patient and insightful editor, Anne Klemm, and to my other friends in the Jane Austen Society of North America, especially Judy Beine, Carrie Bebris, Sara Bowen, Baronda Bradley, Diana Burns, Rosemary Cummings, Liz Philosophos Cooper, Kathy Egstad, Mary Ann Gross, Jeff Heller, Victoria Hinshaw, Marsha Huff, Cynthia Kartman, Cheryl Kinney, Jean Long, Deb Stein, Julie Tynion, and Marylee Wilkinson, who all provided valuable support for this project.

Most importantly, I must thank my husband and children, who now truly understand why authors always thank their families for their patience and support.

Wildflowers in the lanes near Jane Austen's childhood home in Steventon

Introduction

To sit in the shade on a fine day, and look upon verdure,
is the most perfect refreshment.
— *Fanny Price in* Mansfield Park

Jane Austen loved a garden. She took a keen interest in flower gardening and kitchen gardening alike. The Austens grew their own food whenever they could and had flower gardens wherever they lived, at their parsonage garden at Steventon in Hampshire, their town gardens at Bath and Southampton, and when they returned to Hampshire, at their cottage garden at Chawton. In Jane's letters to her sister, Cassandra, we see her planning the details of these family gardens, discussing the planting of fruit, flowers, and trees with enthusiasm. In the course of her life, she also had the opportunity to visit many of the grander gardens of England: her brother's two estates at Chawton and Godmersham, the manor houses of friends and family, and probably even the great estate of Chatsworth, assumed by many to be the inspiration for Pemberley, Darcy's magnificent estate in *Pride and Prejudice*.

Gardens played important roles in all six of her novels. For nearly every house mentioned in the novels there is some sort of garden: Mr. Rushworth's old-fashioned garden and park in *Mansfield Park*, waiting to be "improved"; the parsonage garden of Mr. Collins in *Pride and Prejudice*; or boastful General Tilney's acres of kitchen garden in *Northanger Abbey*. For some of Jane Austen's characters, though, gardens are more than a source of food or flowers, they are places of refuge and spiritual refreshment: Elizabeth Bennet walks in the groves of Rosings to ponder Darcy's letter, Fanny Price finds "animation, both of body and mind" in the gardens of Mansfield Park, and Emma soothes her nerves with a walk in the shrubbery. Jane Austen valued these renewing qualities of a garden herself, writing from her brother's house in London:

> "[T]he Garden is quite a Love. . . . I live in [the] room downstairs, it is
> particularly pleasant, from opening upon the garden. I go & refresh myself
> every now & then, and then come back to Solitary Coolness."
> — Letter from Jane Austen to her sister, Cassandra, 23 August 1814

This book examines the sorts of gardens that Jane Austen would have known and visited: gardens of the great estates, cottage gardens, gardens in town, and public gardens and parks. Using quotations from her novels and letters, gardening and household books of the time, and some of the songs and poetry she loved best, it illustrates for the modern reader how gardens were used and enjoyed by Jane and her contemporaries, and by the characters in her novels.

Some of the gardens Jane owned or knew exist still in some form. These and other restored Georgian and Regency gardens are listed in each chapter, with information on touring them. There is also touring information for some of the estate gardens that are featured in the film adaptations of her novels.

Chawton Cottage, Jane Austen's House Museum

"Oh! what a sweet little cottage"
COTTAGE GARDENS

The garden at Chawton Cottage

*You cannot imagine—it is not in Human Nature to imagine what a nice walk
we have round the Orchard.—The row of Beech look very well indeed, & so
does the young Quickset hedge in the Garden.—I hear today that an Apricot has
been detected on one of the Trees.*

— Letter from Jane Austen at Chawton Cottage, to her sister, Cassandra, 31 May 1811

There is nothing quite like the traditional English cottage garden, that pleasing medley of
flowers, herbs, fruit, and vegetables, a carefree riot of cheerful colors and rich, intoxicating
scents. In Jane Austen's England, cottage gardens came in many sizes and styles. The laborer's
quaint cottage, with its thatched roof and small-paned windows, had a little garden that

As a house, Barton Cottage . . .
was comfortable and compact; but
as a cottage it was defective, for the
building was regular, the roof was
tiled, the window shutters were not
painted green, nor were the walls
covered with honeysuckles.
— *Sense and Sensibility*

combined beauty and usefulness, hollyhocks and herbs, columbines and cabbages. The well-to-do had their own "cottages." The ornamented Uppercross Cottage in *Persuasion* with its "French windows, and other prettiness" was really an elegant house, and its garden would have been equally elegant. Barton Cottage in *Sense and Sensibility* and Jane Austen's own cottage at Chawton fell somewhere in the middle. Chawton Cottage's charming garden contained a kitchen garden and beehives, but it also had a lovely orchard and a shrubbery "very gay with Pinks & Sweet Williams" where Jane and could walk and think, and where the romance of her own English cottage garden surely inspired some of her best work.

Chawton—Peace in a Cottage

Chawton Cottage, where Jane Austen wrote many of her novels, is today a popular museum dedicated to her life and works and hosting thousands of tourists each year. The cottage, a comfortable, rambling house surrounded by shady walks and bright flowers, sits hidden in the tranquil Hampshire countryside. Only an hour's drive from London, the village of Chawton is nevertheless a small, quiet refuge that no doubt looks much as it did in Jane Austen's day. In the summer of 1809, Jane Austen (then 33 years old), her mother, and her sister, Cassandra, returned to Hampshire, to the rural atmosphere Jane loved so much, after an eight-years' absence in Bath and Southampton.

The Austen women had moved from house to house after Jane's father died in 1805, but Chawton Cottage finally provided them with a place worth calling home. Jane's rich brother, Edward Austen Knight, offered his mother and sisters their choice of two houses, at his property in Godmersham, Kent, or at Chawton. They chose Chawton Cottage. The former house of Edward's steward, the cottage was never a "mere laborer's cottage." Set in several acres of pleasant grounds and orchards, the house was well-built and roomy, with six bedrooms, numerous outbuildings, and a good kitchen garden. Edward made many improvements for his mother's and sisters' benefit. He added rooms, bricked up a too-public window overlooking the road in front, and opened another that looked only over the lawn and trees on the garden side of the house. He planted hedges and a shrubbery walk that circled the property, providing a shady place for the Austen women and their friend Martha Lloyd, who lived with them, to stroll in summer, and a dry gravel path for wetter seasons. One of Jane's numerous and fond nieces and nephews, James, recalled the cottage and garden with pleasure:

> A high wooden fence and hornbeam hedge shut out the Winchester road, which skirted the whole length of the little domain. Trees were planted each side to form a shrubbery walk, carried round the enclosure, which gave a sufficient space for ladies' exercise. There was a pleasant irregular mixture of hedgerow, and gravel walk, and orchard, and long grass for mowing, arising from two or three little enclosures having been thrown together. The house itself was quite as good as the generality of parsonage-houses then were, and much in the same style; and was capable of receiving other members of the family as frequent visitors. It was sufficiently well furnished; everything inside and out was kept in good repair, and it was altogether a comfortable and ladylike establishment, though the means which supported it were not large.
>
> — James Edward Austen-Leigh, *Memoir of Jane Austen*

Bee's Wax Lip-Salve

TAKE Yellow Bee's Wax, two ounces and a half; Oil of Sweet Almonds, a quarter of a pint; melt the Wax in the Oil, and let the mixture stand till it become cold, when it acquires a pretty stiff consistence. Scrape it into a marble mortar, and rub it with a wooden pestle, to render it perfectly smooth. Keep it for use in a gallypot, closely covered. It is emollient and lenient; of course good for chaps in the lips, hands, or nipples; and preserves the skin soft and smooth.
— *The Toilet of Flora*, 1779

Jane and her mother and sister enthusiastically set about improving their little domain. They planted the kitchen garden with vegetables and their favorite garden fruits: peas, tomatoes, potatoes, gooseberries, currants, and strawberries among them. "When the Gooseberries are ripe I shall sit upon my Bench, eat them & think of you," wrote Mrs. Austen to a granddaughter. They had fruit trees, in the orchard and trained against the garden walls, including plums and at least one apricot tree (Could it have been a Moor Park apricot, as in *Mansfield Park*?). Cassandra tried her hand at mulberry trees: "I will not say that your Mulberry trees are dead," Jane wrote to her, "but I am afraid that they are not alive."

Much of what the Austens ate came from their garden and orchard. The many years living at Steventon, the parsonage where Jane and Cassandra grew up, had given them expertise in farming matters. They raised turkeys and chickens: "The Chicken are all alive, & fit for

A colorful flower border in the garden at Chawton Cottage

Chawton Cottage

Jane Austen's House Museum
Chawton, Alton, Hampshire
Tel: +44 (0)1420 83262
jane-austens-house-museum.org.uk

The Jane Austen's House Museum is a beautifully restored interpretation of what Chawton Cottage was like when Jane Austen lived there. The attractive gardens contain examples of a working Regency kitchen garden, espaliered fruit trees (trained to grow flat against a wall), a shrubbery, an herb garden, a rose garden, and numerous flower borders. Nearly all the specimens are antique varieties known in the Austens' time or earlier. Inside the cottage, displays include family pictures, china, and furniture, including the little round table on which she composed her novels.

Daisies line the front garden wall of Chawton Cottage.

the Table—but we save them for something grand," Jane reported to Cassandra. Bees, which fed on the flowers and fruit trees in their garden, provided honey: "I am happy to hear of the Honey.—I was thinking of it the other day," wrote Jane. The honey was made into mead, a delicious, fermented beverage that was a staple in the Austen household. "I long to know something of the Mead," Jane wrote to Cassandra, and another time: "We must husband our present stock of Mead—& I am sorry to perceive that our 20 Gal: is very nearly out.—I cannot comprehend how the 14 Gal: c[oul]d last so long."

Jane and her family also delighted in filling their garden with flowers and flowering bushes, collecting seeds and roots from family and friends for the shrubbery and flower borders. The shrubbery, an airy gravel walk winding through trees and shrubs, became a pleasant, blooming spot:

Our young Piony at the foot of the Fir tree has just blown &
looks very handsome; & the whole of the Shrubbery Border
will soon be very gay with Pinks & Sweet Williams, in addition
to the Columbines already in bloom. The Syringas too are
coming out.
— Letter from Jane Austen to Cassandra, 29 May 1811

Chawton Cottage and its garden turned out to be just what Jane needed.
Her lively letters, reporting her obvious pleasure in her new surroundings,
hint that she had found again the environment she needed to be
productive and happy. Austen family tradition reports that in her first
year at Chawton, she revised both *Sense and Sensibility* and *Pride and Prejudice*
(her most famous book) to prepare them for publication. *Northanger Abbey*
was revised there as well, and *Mansfield Park*, *Emma*, and *Persuasion* were all
written entirely at Chawton.

The True Cottage Garden

Romantic notions of sweet, vine-covered cottages, simple and surrounded
by nature, occupied the imaginations of the gentry of Jane Austen's day.
The simple, thatched cottage held an honored place in the sort of gothic
romance novels that Jane Austen so loved to lampoon. Popular authors
such as Ann Radcliffe and Anna Maria Porter waxed lyrical about the
charms of living in a such a cottage. Impoverished romantic heroines were
not deprived, it seemed; living the pure peasant life actually enhanced
their charms. Even Isabella Thorpe, the shallow friend of Catherine
Morland, the heroine of *Northanger Abbey* (Jane Austen's humorous send-
up of the gothic romance genre), claims that love in a cottage would be
enough for her:

> "For my own part," said Isabella, "my wishes are so moderate
> that the smallest income in nature would be enough for me.
> Where people are really attached, poverty itself is wealth;
> grandeur I detest: I would not settle in London for the
> universe. A cottage in some retired village would be ecstasy."

But then she betrays herself by adding, "There are some charming little villas about Richmond."
Richmond, an upscale suburb of London, certainly had charming villas, but they were hardly
the sort of dwellings where one lived simply.

Rough farm laborers and their families rather than flaxen-haired heroines inhabited the
true simple cottage. In Jane Austen's day, a great deal of the agricultural land was held by estate
owners such as Jane's brother Edward Austen Knight and, fictionally, Mr. Darcy in *Pride and*

Prejudice. Often owning many thousands of acres, including entire villages such as Chawton, these gentlemen derived most of their wealth from rents. Cottagers were usually desperately poor, living day to day, and easily overset by sickness or bad luck. In *Emma*, the story of a misguided matchmaker, the well-off heroine and her friend Harriet Smith make a charitable visit to some ill cottagers, as all good gentlewomen were supposed to do. Jane Austen gives us an idea of what a real cottage and its garden looked like:

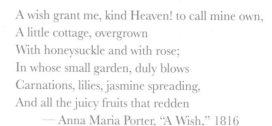

A wish grant me, kind Heaven! to call mine own,
A little cottage, overgrown
With honeysuckle and with rose;
In whose small garden, duly blows
Carnations, lilies, jasmine spreading,
And all the juicy fruits that redden
— Anna Maria Porter, "A Wish," 1816

> Emma was very compassionate; and the distresses of the poor were as sure of relief from her personal attention and kindness, her counsel and her patience, as from her purse. . . . In the present instance, it was sickness and poverty together which she came to visit; and . . . she quitted the cottage with such an impression of the scene as made her say to Harriet, as they walked away,
>
> "These are the sights, Harriet, to do one good. How trifling they make every thing else appear! . . .
>
> "And really, I do not think the impression will soon be over," said Emma, as she crossed the low hedge, and tottering footstep which ended the narrow, slippery path through the cottage garden, and brought them into the lane again. "I do not think it will," stopping to look once more at all the outward wretchedness of the place, and recall the still greater within.

Agriculture experts and essayists urged landowners to improve the living conditions of their laborers by building them comfortable cottages with useful attached gardens. Perhaps recognizing the futility of appealing to some people's nonexistent good natures, they worked on the estate owners' selfish instincts. Improved conditions meant better workers, they claimed, and anyway, a nice cottage was pretty to look at.

It was hard to judge, experts said, just how big a laborer's cottage garden should be. Too small, and it would not help support his family; too large a garden, and it led to perilous thoughts of independence on the worker's part. John Loudon, the famous garden designer, proposed his vision of the ideal worker's cottage, humanely planned to consider the needs and comfort of the laborer. An excellent garden, stocked by the estate owner, should be attached to it, he said:

> In *the Garden should be a Well,* . . . A *Water-Closet* [privy] placed in a hidden part of the garden, . . . A Pigstye, . . . A *Dunghill,* . . . two or more beehives. . . . The

In the Garden with Jane Austen

The demonstration dye plant garden at Chawton Cottage occupies a former 20th-century rose garden.

surrounding fence may be a wall, close pales, a holly, thorn, sloe-thorn, or damson-plum hedge, . . . if a hedge of any kind, then standard plum, pear, apple, or cherry trees, may be planted in it; if a wall, the same sorts may be trained against it. . . .

The quarters may be surrounded with a line of gooseberries and currants, and a few standard apples or plums, (as being the two most useful cottage fruits,) scattered over the whole. Against the house may be planted currants, pears, or a [grape]vine, according to the situation and climate. Honeysuckles and monthly roses may be planted next the porch; ivy against the water-closet; and the scented climatis against the pigstye. The border round the house should be devoted to savory pot-herbs, as parsley, thyme, mint, chives, &c. and to flowers, and low flowering shrubs. The surrounding border under the wall or hedge, should be devoted to early and late culinary crops, as early potatoes, pease, turnips, kidney-beans, &c.

— *An Encyclopaedia of Gardening*, 1822

Farm and Parsonage Gardens

The gardens at farms and parsonages represented a considerable step up from the true cottage garden. These gardens contained many of the features of a cottage garden, the main purpose of which was the production of fruits and vegetables for the family, but how ornate the gardens were after that depended on the social status and social aspirations of the owners.

In *Emma*, Robert Martin rents his large farm from Mr. Knightley, the hero of the story. Robert has genteel aspirations, but although he is a good-hearted, "respectable, intelligent gentleman farmer," according to Mr. Knightley, and although he is wealthy enough to have two maids and to send his sisters to Mrs. Goddard's school in Highbury, he still lacks polish enough to suit Emma. Indeed his garden is a mixture of the practical and the would-be elegant. The front garden of his farmhouse is a useful rather than a purely decorative garden, with a neat white gate and espaliered fruit trees lining the walk. Perhaps it is his sisters who have instituted at least one fashionable garden feature: Emma's friend Harriet, always easily impressed, breathlessly reports to Emma that Mr. Martin has "a very handsome summer house in their garden, where some day next year they were all to drink tea—a very handsome summer house, large enough to hold a dozen people."

Parsonage gardens often had more elegant features in addition to the practical, food-producing areas found at farmhouses, as parsons were almost invariably drawn from the educated and upper classes and could be expected to want their properties to reflect their refined backgrounds. Each of the many thousands of parishes in England required a parson, either a rector or a vicar, who generally lived in his parish, though some parsons (such as Jane Austen's father) ministered to the needs of more than one parish. Each parish usually had a parsonage, a house for the parson, sometimes modest, but often large and comfortable. Parsonages were often attached to the farmlands of the "living" to which the parson was appointed. The mixture of farm income and tithes (usually 10 percent of farm production in the parish) literally provided the rector with his living, as he received no other salary. Vicars, however, held their livings vicariously, receiving a stipend only, and were often poor as a result. Jane Austen's father, a rector, held the livings of Steventon and Deane, which came with two farms to help support his family. As livings went, they weren't bad—the Austens lived a fairly comfortable life, never entirely free from worry, but never really very poor. Many of Jane Austen's characters are men of the cloth: Dr. Grant and Edmund Bertram in *Mansfield Park*, Henry Tilney in *Northanger Abbey*, Edward Ferrars in *Sense and Sensibility*, Mr. Elton in *Emma*, and, of course, that deliciously pompous ninny, Mr. Collins, in *Pride and Prejudice*. We don't hear of most of them working in their gardens, but Mr. Collins does, much to his wife's pleasure:

> Mr. Collins invited them to take a stroll in the garden, which was large and well laid out, and to the cultivation of which he attended himself. To work in this garden was one of his most respectable pleasures; and Elizabeth admired the command of countenance with which Charlotte talked of the healthfulness of the exercise, and owned she encouraged it as much as possible.

Stubbs Farm

Stubbs Farm

South Hay, Kingsley, Hampshire
Tel: +44 (0)1420 474906
stubbsfarm.co.uk

Very near Chawton lies Stubbs Farm, a working farm
dating from the sixteenth century. The buildings and
farmyard give an idea of what a farm in Jane Austen's
day must have looked like. Bed and breakfast and self-
catering accommodations available. Grounds and walks
open to guests.

The other parsons in Jane Austen's novels, all gentlemen's sons, may not work in their gardens personally, but they busy themselves with planning improvements to their properties, adding fashionable elements such as shrubberies (plantings of shrubs and trees through which gravel walks wound their way) and sweeps (circular driveways), in imitation of the smaller houses of the gentry. In style, such an improved farm was essentially a *ferme ornée*, or ornamented farm, where shrubberies and walks led around meadows and fields.

Henry Tilney, the delightful, amusing parson in *Northanger Abbey*, has aspirations for improving his parsonage grounds. The heroine, Catherine Morland, visits her beloved Henry's parsonage and is delighted with the view from the drawing room window, crying, "Oh! what a sweet little cottage there is among the trees—apple trees too! It is the prettiest cottage!" Her comments draw the attention of Henry's arrogant father, General Tilney, embarrassing her, but a tour of Henry's pleasure grounds restores her calm:

> The influence of fresh objects and fresh air, however, was of great use in dissipating these embarrassing associations; and, having reached the ornamental part of the premises, consisting of a walk round two sides of a meadow, on which Henry's genius had begun to act about half a year ago, she was sufficiently recovered to think it prettier than any pleasure ground she had ever been in before, though there was not a shrub in it higher than the green bench in the corner.

Mrs. Grant, the parson's wife in *Mansfield Park*, has greatly improved the pleasure grounds of the parsonage there. The mild heroine, Fanny Price, always attuned to the beauties of nature, is full of admiration for the changes. Mrs. Grant's sister, sophisticated, city-bred Mary Crawford, is surprised that it exists at all:

"This is pretty, very pretty," said Fanny, looking around her as they were thus sitting together one day; "every time I come into this shrubbery I am more struck with its growth and beauty. Three years ago, this was nothing but a rough hedgerow along the upper side of the field, never thought of as anything, or capable of becoming anything; and now it is converted into a walk, and it would be

On her return to Crankhumdunberry (of which sweet village her father was Rector), Charlotte was received with the greatest Joy by Frederic & Elfrida, who, after pressing her alternately to their Bosoms, proposed to her to take a walk in a Grove of Poplars which led from the Parsonage to a verdant Lawn enamelled with a variety of variegated flowers & watered by a purling Stream, brought from the Valley of Tempé by a passage under ground.

— "Frederic & Elfrida," written by Jane Austen as a teenager

A flower border grows along a rustic fence at Stubbs Farm.

difficult to say whether most valuable as a convenience or an ornament
. . . . There is such a quiet simplicity in the plan of the walk! Not too much
attempted!"

"Yes," replied Miss Crawford carelessly, "it does very well for a place of this
sort. One does not think of extent here; and between ourselves, till I came to
Mansfield, I had not imagined a country parson ever aspired to a shrubbery, or
anything of the kind."

Plucking a Rose

Barns, brewhouses, chicken coops, granaries, and bakehouses were all among the many
unattractive, though useful, outbuildings found in a country garden, but none was so useful or
so necessary as the privy. Jane Austen doesn't mention such ordinary, everyday structures in her
novels or letters, but, naturally, every house had one. True water closets, attached to or inside
the house, were a rarity in the country in Jane's time. Whether sunny or snowy, the options were
limited: the chamber pot or the garden. Back in the back of the garden, understandably as far
away from the house as possible, stood the "conveniency" or "necessary house." The simple
ones were similar to a modern privy at a cabin in the woods: a hut made of simple boards over
a deep hole. Outhouse fashions haven't changed very much since: woodcuts and drawings of
the time show the traditional half-moon or heart cutout in the door. When the time came to
change the location of the outhouse, the old spot was considered a good one to plant a fruit tree.
Grander houses built grander privies, sometimes made of stone or brick, and often disguised as

The site of Steventon Rectory is now a field.

Steventon

Steventon is on the B3400/Worting Road, about 8 miles from Basingstoke. The easiest way to find St. Nicholas Church and the site of the former parsonage is to drive to the village and ask for directions.

An engraving of Steventon Rectory from A Memoir of Jane Austen, *1871, based on a drawing by Jane Austen's niece Anna.*

In the Garden with Jane Austen

a decorative garden feature. The inevitable outings to the garden, great or small, made the term "plucking a rose" synonymous with a trip to the outhouse, reminiscent of our "Excuse me, I have to powder my nose."

Bellflower

Steventon

Jane Austen's love of living in the country came from the years she spent growing up at her father's parsonage at Steventon, a small village set in the beautiful green Hampshire countryside. The area surrounding Steventon has a quiet, pastoral beauty, with narrow lanes bordered by ancient hedgerows and flower-filled meadows. Pulled down not long after Jane's death, the Austen parsonage stood at the corner of the bottom of the shady lane leading up to her father's church, St. Nicholas. The church, which dates to Norman times (it was originally constructed around 1200), still stands, guarded by a towering yew tree possibly dating to the same period. The church looks somewhat different from how it appeared when Jane Austen worshiped there, with a Victorian spire tacked on to the top of the square Norman tower and some interior changes in decoration, but otherwise it is substantially the same. Artifacts found on the site of the parsonage are on display in the church, including the old pump from the Austens' well, and remains of metal pattens, clogs with metal rings that were worn to keep women's shoes up out of the mud.

Not content with a mere old-fashioned parsonage, the Austens made many improvements to their property. There was a modern sweep, and what Jane Austen called the "Elm Walk" was planted with flowering hawthorn and lilacs as a rustic shrubbery, complete with occasional seats. The Austens had a fine garden in the back of the house, sloping up the hill to a green turfed terrace (remains of which can still be seen). At the eastern end of the terrace began the "Church Walk," a path that ran up the steep hill to the church between hedgerows, Jane's nephew James reported, under whose shelter "the earliest primroses, anemones, and wild hyacinths were to be found." In the large, old-fashioned walled garden, the Austens grew a mixture of vegetables, fruits, and flowers. Mr. Austen's study overlooked the garden, Jane's niece Anna said:

> The lower bow-window, which looked so cheerfully into the sunny garden and up the middle grass walk bordered with strawberries, to the sundial at the end, was that of my grandfather's study, his own exclusive property, safe from the bustle of all household cares.

Traces of the Austens' residence could be seen for many years after the destruction of the house. The grass grew sparsely where the gravel drive had been, and flowers continued to bloom here and there over the original garden until the late 1800s. The site is now a field.

The Cottage Ornée

Ox-Eye Daisies

The wealthy of Jane Austen's day had the romantic notion that any countryside house smaller than a mansion must necessarily be a cottage, and they carried that idea to extremes, building a highly ornamented type of elegant villa called the cottage ornée. The gardens of a cottage ornée bore almost no resemblance to a true cottage garden. Though often set on relatively small properties, sometimes just a few acres, they generally possessed many of the garden features of the larger estates, such as ornamental flower gardens, conservatories, and shrubberies. The kitchen garden and other practical areas would usually have been hidden behind the house, preferably screened by walls or trees and bushes. If we judge by the characters in her novels, Jane Austen seems not to have been impressed by the "cottages" of the rich. In *Sanditon* (one of her unfinished novels), Sir Edward Denham, a foolish man who fancies himself a rake, "is running up a tasteful little cottage ornée" to rent to lodgers in a seaside resort. In *Sense and Sensibility*, the equally foolish and self-satisfied Robert Ferrars chatters at length to Elinor Dashwood about his vision of life in a simple country cottage:

> "For my own part," said he, "I am excessively fond of a cottage; there is always so much comfort, so much elegance about them. And I protest, if I had any money to spare, I should buy a little land and build one myself, within a short distance of London, where I might drive myself down at any time, and collect a few friends about me, and be happy."

In fact, what he is really describing is an elegant, expensive retreat. Any garden there would doubtless be elegant and expensive as well.

Houghton Lodge

Within an easy drive of Chawton sits a beautifully preserved example of the late-eighteenth-century cottage ornée style, Houghton Lodge. The lodge (a private residence) and its gardens are open for tours. The interior has been tastefully restored, and features many delightfully ornate examples of the style, including fantasy gothic woodwork inside and pointed gothic windows that run down to the ground, reminiscent of "Uppercross Cottage, with its veranda, French windows, and other prettiness," Charles and Mary Musgrove's cottage in *Persuasion*.

The pleasure grounds and gardens are extensive, and include a shrubbery leading to a grotto, a topiary boxwood garden, and a walled kitchen garden that also houses a state-of-the-art hydroponic garden, the Hydroponicum, in its greenhouse.

The Topiary Peacock Garden at Houghton Lodge

Houghton Lodge & Gardens

Stockbridge, Hampshire
Tel: +44 (0)1264 810502
Tel +44 (0) 1264 810912 recorded
admission information
houghtonlodge.co.uk

Houghton Lodge, an excellent example of the eighteenth-century gothic cottage ornée style, is set on the scenic banks of the River Test. The Lodge has often hosted film crews, including such BBC productions as *David Copperfield, Wilde,* and *The Buccaneers.* The extensive grounds and gardens have been restored to a late-eighteenth-century appearance and feature wildlife walks through the water meadows along the river, a woodland walk leading to a grotto, a walled garden, flower borders, a hydroponic garden, an orchid house, and examples of topiary, including the Topiary Peacock Garden and a topiary dragon. Tours of the interior of the house are by appointment.

The lake and Vanbrugh's Grand Bridge at Blenheim Palace

"From every window there were beauties to be seen"

MANSION & MANOR HOUSE GARDENS

The River Stour flows through Godmersham Park, Kent.

The eye was instantly caught by Pemberley House . . . . It was a large,
handsome stone building, standing well on rising ground, and backed by a ridge
of high woody hills; and in front, a stream of some natural importance was
swelled into greater, but without any artificial appearance. Its banks were neither
formal nor falsely adorned. Elizabeth was delighted.
— Pride and Prejudice

What could be more inspiring to the imagination than the grandeur and beauty of Pemberley? In *Pride and Prejudice*, Elizabeth Bennet tours Darcy's vast estate with delight and perhaps with a touch of regret that she had turned down his marriage proposal. The exquisitely landscaped grounds and gardens of Pemberley, where "from every window there were beauties to be seen," represent the very best of the grand English

In the Garden with Jane Austen

landscape garden style. Great estates in Jane Austen's day were showplaces for the wealth and power of the British elite, with beautiful parkland filled with magnificent tree-lined avenues, grottoes, classically inspired temples, bridges, and columns, and acres of gardens. In novel after novel, Jane Austen's characters' lives and loves are interwoven with their estates: "dear, dear Norland" in *Sense and Sensibility*; Hartfield and Donwell Abbey in *Emma*, Mansfield Park and Northanger Abbey in the novels of the same names, Kellynch Hall in *Persuasion*; and Longbourn, Netherfield, and, of course that greatest of all fictional estates, Pemberley, in *Pride and Prejudice*.

Pemberley and the Great Estates

Fitzwilliam Darcy, one of the all-time great romantic heroes, is one of Jane Austen's most beloved creations. A fabulously wealthy man, he owns Pemberley, a magnificent estate rivaled only by the very largest of the great English estates. Jane Austen tells us that the park at Pemberley is "ten miles round," putting the estate in the same category as Chatsworth (thought by many to be the inspiration for Pemberley), which was nine miles in circumference, and Blenheim Palace, the grounds of which (according to guidebooks of the time) were 11 or 12 miles around. Such great estates had huge gardens. Blenheim's gardens covered 200 acres, (including eight acres devoted to the kitchen gardens alone), with ornamental temples, bridges, water cascades, flower gardens nestled in a wooded grove, and sheltered walks "between clumps and groups of the most luxuriant and delicate trees of various climes, intermixed with flowers and shrubs of the utmost fragrance and beauty." Pemberley's gardens, we can imagine, might have rivaled Blenheim's.

Godmersham Park

Jane Austen's brother Edward was a lucky man. Rich, childless cousins, the Knights, took a fancy to Edward, the Austens' third son, and made him their heir. He ultimately inherited two large estates from the Knights, Godmersham Park in Kent and Chawton House in Hampshire, changing his name to Knight on coming into the property in 1812. "I must learn to make a better K," Jane wrote to Cassandra that November.

Godmersham Park (also said to have been a possible inspiration for Pemberley), is located among the beautiful wooded hills and downs near Canterbury. In Jane Austen's time it possessed a large park and extensive pleasure grounds. Set in the pretty valley watered by the River Stour, Godmersham was often featured in collections of "engravings of gentlemen's seats." The engravings show deer, cattle, and sheep grazing in the park in front of a low, handsome house (which still stands),with a central section containing the entrance hall, flanked by two wings. One of the wings, which unfortunately has had its interior altered beyond recognition, had a large and comfortable library, where Jane liked to write during her lengthy visits to Edward and his family. Jane and Cassandra Austen each spent months at a time visiting at Godmersham, and Jane particularly relished the luxurious life there in contrast to the constant scrimping of life at Chawton Cottage.

The gardens and shrubberies of Godmersham lay in the back of the house, on the southern side, sloping up a hill to a planted wood, called "Bentigh." There, Edward Austen Knight planted an avenue of trees. Jane's great-nephew, Edward, 1st Lord Brabourne, described the southern grounds:

> "Bentigh" was once a ploughed field, but when my grandfather first came to Godmersham he planted it with underwood, and made gravel walks through it, planted an avenue of trees on each side of the principal walk, and added it to the shrubberies. The family always walked through it on their way to church, leaving the shrubberies by a little door in the wall, at the end of the private grounds, which brought them out just opposite the church.

In the front of the house, across the river, on its east side, grew another wood, called "Temple Plantations," for the little summerhouse in the form of a temple there (which still stands). Jane enjoyed strolling all over Godmersham Park:

> Yesterday passed quite *a la* Godmersham: the gentlemen rode about Edward's farm, and returned in time to saunter along Bentigh with us; and after dinner we visited the Temple Plantations, which, to be sure, is a Chevalier Bayard of a plantation. James and Mary are much struck with the beauty of the place.
> — Letter from Jane Austen to Cassandra, 16 June 1808

Jane must have thought the trees of Temple Plantations quite beautiful: the Chevalier Bayard, the greatest knight of France, was always depicted in engravings of his adventures as lying under a large, noble tree during his glorious death scene.

Remnants of the gardens and shrubberies still exist at Godmersham. The extensive walled kitchen gardens remain, now filled with flower gardens. Woods grow in the locations of Temple Plantations and Bentigh, though the avenue of trees in Bentigh blew down in the great windstorm of 1987. An new avenue of lime trees (lindens) have been planted in their place.

Godmersham Park is in private ownership and is open only by special arrangement.

Chawton House

Edward Austen Knight's second large estate, Chawton House, is located in Hampshire, in the same village where Jane and Cassandra Austen and their mother lived in one of his properties, Chawton Cottage. Edward and his family often stayed at Chawton House, an attractive Elizabethan manor, for months at a time, in summers, or when Godmersham was being painted. Jane's niece Fanny recorded the daily visiting between the cottage and the Great House in her diaries: "We drank tea at the Cottage" and "The Cottage dined here" were frequent entries. She

The walled kitchen garden at Chawton House

Chawton House

Chawton, Hampshire
Tel: +44 (0)1420 541010
chawtonhouse.org

Chawton House, a warm brick house dating to Elizabethan times, is an easy stroll from Jane Austen's House Museum. The house, formerly owned by Jane Austen's brother Edward, is now home to the Chawton House Library. The grounds and gardens are currently being carefully restored, mostly to their late-eighteenth- and early-nineteenth-century appearance. The Library Terrace and Upper Terrace gardens, which show the influence of Sir Edwin Lutyens, are being restored to their early twentieth-century form in the style of Gertrude Jekyll. Garden features include a walled kitchen garden, a lime (linden) avenue, a fernery, and a wilderness. Self-guided tours of the gardens may be taken on weekdays. Guided tours of the house and library are available on certain days each month; booking ahead is recommended.

recorded also the many walks she and her aunts took in the pleasant grounds of Chawton House.

Today the house contains the Chawton House Library, a center for the study of the works and lives of women writers who wrote before 1830. The gardens and pleasure grounds at Chawton House (open certain days each month) today look nearly the same as they did at the end of the eighteenth century, complete with a wilderness walk, a lime (linden) avenue, and a ha-ha (a sunken fence), though there are some attractive Edwardian terraced additions to the garden. Jane Austen did not live to see one of Edward's additions, a walled kitchen garden that sits at the top of the rise behind the house, though she knew it was planned. The kitchen garden is gradually being restored according to the original planting plan.

"A park, a real park"

"Every park has its beauty and its prospects," Jane Austen tells us. Many of the great estates in her novels are parks: Norland Park and Barton Park in *Sense and Sensibility*, Netherfield Park and Rosings Park in *Pride and Prejudice*, and Mansfield Park, in the novel of the same name. Mansfield, one day to be inherited by Tom Bertram, is smaller than Pemberley, though would still be considered quite large. Worldly Mary Crawford, contemplating marriage with Tom, is impressed:

> Miss Crawford soon felt that he and his situation might do. She looked about her with due consideration, and found almost everything in his favour: a park, a real park, five miles round, a spacious modern built house, so well placed and well screened as to deserve to be in any collection of engravings of gentlemen's seats in the kingdom, and wanting only to be completely new furnished . . . .

The "real park" that so fascinates Mary Crawford is a deer park (an estate where deer were kept for the hunting pleasure of the upper classes), usually found only on the older, larger estates. Deer parks, the possession of which was originally a royal prerogative, could be enclosed only with a direct grant from the monarch, and to own one implied that desirable quality, old money. Most country estates, such as Cleveland, the estate where the heroines, Elinor and Marianne Dashwood, visit their acquaintances, the Palmers, in *Sense and Sensibility*, lacked a true park:

> Cleveland was a spacious, modern built house, situated on a sloping lawn. It had no park, but the pleasure grounds were tolerably extensive; and like every other place of the same degree of importance, it had its open shrubbery, and closer wood walk, a road of smooth gravel winding round a plantation, led to the front, the lawn was dotted over with timber, the house itself was under the guardianship of the fir, the mountain ash, and the acacia, and a thick screen of them altogether, interspersed with tall Lombardy poplars, shut out the offices.

Blenheim Palace

Woodstock, Oxfordshire
Tel: +44 (0)8700 60 20 80
blenheimpalace.com

Blenheim Palace, a World Heritage Site, is home to
the 11th Duke of Marlborough and is the birthplace
of Sir Winston Churchill. Situated in the heart of the
Oxfordshire Cotswolds, the Palace is surrounded by over
2,000 acres of "Capability" Brown landscaped park
and breathtaking formal gardens, including the Rose
Garden, the Secret Garden, the Italian Gardens, and the
Water Terraces.

Chatsworth House

Bakewell, Derbyshire
Tel: +44 (0)1246 565300
chatsworth.org

Home to the Duke and Duchess of Devonshire, the grand estate of Chatsworth is supposed by many to be Jane Austen's inspiration for Pemberley. The Pemberley scenes for the 2005 film version of *Pride and Prejudice* (starring Keira Knightley and Matthew Macfadyen) were in fact filmed at Chatsworth. There are five miles of walks leading through the 105 acres of celebrated gardens, which include formal gardens, a rock garden, a kitchen garden, a cottage garden, and a sensory garden.

The Improvement of the Estate

Many in the upper classes lived year-round on their estates, but others spent only part of the year there, called to London by the parliamentary session and the social season. Most of the gentry welcomed the seasonal return to the countryside, to rest and rural recreation, and even those landowners who enjoyed spending half their year in London valued their estates for the income and status having an estate gave. Landowners often spent a great deal of their time managing and improving their properties, striving to better their incomes and enhance the appearance of their estates. By Jane Austen's day, the earlier fashion for geometric styles of gardening and landscaping (which copied the European styles exemplified by the gardens at Versailles) had all but died in Great Britain. A preference for the romantic and the picturesque in art and fiction led gradually to a distaste for artificial forms in garden and landscape design, forms that came to be associated with the corrupt decadence of the repressive monarchies of Europe. The new style of the English landscape garden was thought to represent British liberty and the purity of nature, and owners such as Mr. Rushworth in *Mansfield Park* were eager to "improve" their estates to meet the new standards:

As gardening is not an inventive art, but an imitation of nature, or rather nature itself ornamented; it follows necessarily, that every thing unnatural ought to be rejected with disdain. Statues of wild beasts vomiting water, a common ornament in gardens, prevails in those of Versailles. Is this ornament in a good taste ? . . . [A] representation of what really exists in nature, admits not any unnatural circumstance.
— Henry Home, *Elements of Criticism*, 1762

> Mr. Rushworth . . . was now making his appearance at Mansfield for the first time since the Crawfords' arrival. He had been visiting a friend in the neighbouring county, and that friend having recently had his grounds laid out by an improver, Mr. Rushworth was returned with his head full of the subject, and very eager to be improving his own place in the same way; and though not saying much to the purpose, could talk of nothing else.
>
> "I wish you could see Compton," said he; "it is the most complete thing! I never saw a place so altered in my life. I told Smith I did not know where I was. The approach *now,* is one of the finest things in the country: you see the house in the most surprising manner. I declare, when I got back to Sotherton yesterday, it looked like a prison—quite a dismal old prison."

Early in the movement, anything that looked artificial was considered automatically undesirable. When the early landscape designers, among them William Kent and Lancelot "Capability" Brown, were unleashed on the great estates of Britain, they felled ancient, symmetrical avenues of trees, uprooted labyrinths and flower beds wholesale, and banished anything that seemed man-made from the landscape. The irony was that the ultimate result was just as much an artificial production as what it replaced, with whole hills raised or leveled to obtain proper vistas, manufactured lakes carefully placed to reflect the new surroundings, and even entire villages moved to accommodate a landowner's artistic vision.

Kent, Brown, and other early improvers removed so much in the way of ornament from the landscape that the effect was rather bald, with houses rising abruptly from smooth, bare lawns decorated only with clumps of trees. People complained. "Our virtuosi have scarcely left an acre of shade, or three trees growing in a line, from the Land's End to the Tweed," said Sir William Chambers, who favored a more ornate style.

By the time Jane Austen was writing her novels, a more deliberately decorative style of landscaping was considered acceptable, even desirable. In *Mansfield Park*, Mr. Rushworth hopes to hire Humphry Repton (considered one of the greatest English landscape designers), who designed the grounds at Stoneleigh Abbey, Jane Austen's cousin's estate. Mr. Rushworth will make a wise choice if he does, because Repton allowed useful and attractive features such as shrubberies, terraces, and flower beds near the house in his landscape designs, which combined "all that was excellent in the former schools" and were "the union of an artistical knowledge of the subject with good taste and good sense," according to John Loudon, a later landscape designer. Pemberley, Darcy's house in *Pride and Prejudice*, has had its grounds improved to precisely the correct degree, as Elizabeth Bennet thinks:

> She had never seen a place for which nature had done more, or where natural beauty had been so little counteracted by an awkward taste. They were all of them warm in their admiration; and at that moment she felt that to be mistress of Pemberley might be something!

The Pleasure Grounds of the Estate

The parks of the larger estates generally were used for timber, deer, and livestock, including cattle and sheep. But they also had smaller, decoratively planted areas, the pleasure grounds, closer to the house, solely for the use of the people who lived there. Pleasure grounds often included wooded walks, perhaps leading to temples, hermitages, and other structures meant for inspiration and sitting in quiet contemplation, and, closer yet to the house, shrubberies with their flowering plants and drier walks, lawns, flower gardens, conservatories, and hothouses. The pleasure grounds of the estate were separated from the park, sometimes with fences, but the preferred method was to use that great innovation of the early improvers of the estate: the ha-ha, a sunken fence that preserved the view from the house while keeping the livestock off the lawn.

The Flower Garden

Closest to the house, often surrounding it, were the flower gardens of the estate. By the nineteenth century, fashion allowed many styles, as the preference of the owners dictated.

> As subjects of fancy and taste, the styles of flower-gardens are various. The modern style is a collection of irregular

> I would have everything as complete as possible in the country, shrubberies and flower gardens, and rustic seats innumerable.
> —Mary Crawford in *Mansfield Park*

groups and masses, placed about the house as a medium, uniting it with the open lawn. The ancient geometric style, in place of irregular groups, employed symmetrical forms; in France, adding statues and fountains; in Holland, cut trees and grassy slopes; and in Italy, stone-walls, walled-terraces, and flights of steps. In some situations, these characteristics of parterres may with propriety be added to, or used instead of the modern sort.
— *An Encyclopaedia of Gardening*, 1822

Many designers did favor the "ancient geometric style"; the flatter areas around a house lent themselves especially well to terraces, intricately patterned flower beds, and formal paths. The "modern" style was further subdivided into two types: flowers grown in beds edged with box or flowers such as pinks, and flowers grown in clumps and beds on the lawn. A general style prevailed in some gardens, with a mixture of flowers providing successive bloom over the entire season. Other gardens had themes. Possibilities included seasonal gardens (evergreen winter gardens were popular), bulb gardens, Dutch, French, or Italian gardens, gardens imitating those of ancient Greece or exotic China, and even American gardens, where the plants were usually grown in "bog earth" (acidic soil), as American plants were generally thought to be lime-intolerant.

Flower beds also could be scattered in the shrubbery and on the lawn. If placed in the shrubbery, the best effect was achieved when paths opened suddenly upon them, providing a surprising and pleasing view. Beds carved out of the lawn often were surrounded by "baskets," decorative edgings of wrought iron or wood made to look like the sides of baskets.

Paths in the flower garden were nearly always of rolled gravel with planted edgings:

Thrift is the neatest small evergreen next to box. In other parts, the daisy, pink, London-pride, primrose, violet, and periwinkle, may be employed as edgings. The strawberry, with the runners cut-in close during summer, will also have a good effect; the wood-strawberry is suitable under the spreading shade of trees. Lastly, the limits between the gravel-walks and the dug-work may sometimes be marked by running verges of grass kept close and neat.
— *An Encyclopaedia of Gardening*, 1822

"One likes to get out into a shrubbery"

Shrubberies, walks near the house through carefully arranged trees and shrubs, were essential and beautiful parts of the pleasure grounds of the estate. Attractive places in themselves, they had health benefits as well, people thought. Of all the threats to life and health in Georgian and Regency Britain, smallpox, consumption (tuberculosis), and other untreatable infectious diseases were probably most dreaded. But as an everyday preoccupation, fear of dampness loomed large. Wet feet could kill, people thought, and women, with their flimsy shoes and supposedly fragile constitutions, ran the most risk. The climate in Great Britain, famous for its frequent rain, made exercise difficult in the countryside: paths and lanes often turned into muddy quagmires not fit for walking in. In *Emma*, Mr. Woodhouse fears dampness even for the robust Mr. Knightley when he sees he has been walking after a rain shower. "But you must have found it very damp and dirty," he tells George Knightley. "I wish you may not catch cold." More distressing to him, though, is the news that Jane Fairfax (determined to pick up her love letters at the post office) has been walking in the rain:

> "I am very sorry to hear, Miss Fairfax, of your being out this morning in the rain. Young ladies should take care of themselves.—Young ladies are delicate plants. They should take care of their health and their complexion. My dear, did you change your stockings?"
> "Yes, sir, I did indeed; and I am very much obliged by your kind solicitude about me."

Shrubberies, with their quick-draining gravel walks, were the perfect answer to the British climate, and indeed they came to be seen as almost a mandatory component of a country estate's pleasure grounds. In *Mansfield Park*, the indolent Lady Bertram values a shrubbery on the occasional days when she can summon up enough energy to go outdoors. She advises Mr. Rushworth to plant a shrubbery when he improves his estate, Sotherton Court:

> "Mr. Rushworth," said Lady Bertram, "if I were you, I would have a very pretty shrubbery. One likes to get out into a shrubbery in fine weather."

If possible, estate owners laid out the walks of the shrubbery in lengths sufficient to provide real exercise. The ideal shrubbery began conveniently near at the house, and wound through and around the estate pleasure grounds, leading to various viewpoints and seats, then circling back to the house. The circuit could be repeated as many times as needed to supply the proper amount of exercise. Several walks were often laid out, for variety and to provide options for the length of the stroll. In *Emma*, Mr. Woodhouse's estate, Hartfield, has "two divisions of the ground" which "sufficed him for his long walk, or his short,

Pot Pourri.

Put into a large China jar the following ingredients in layers, with bay-salt strewed between the layers, two pecks of damask roses, part in buds and part blown; violets, orange-flowers, and jasmine, a, handful of each; orris-root sliced, benjamin and storax, two ounces of each; a quarter of an ounce of musk; a quarter of a pound of angelica-root sliced; a quart of the red parts of clove-gillyflowers; two handfuls of lavender-flowers; half a handful of rosemary-flowers; bay and laurel leaves, half a handful of each; three Seville oranges, stuck as full of cloves as possible, dried in a cool oven, and pounded; half a handful of knotted marjoram; and two handfuls of balm of Gilead dried. Cover all quite close. When the pot is uncovered the perfume is very fine.
— Maria Rundell, *A New System of Domestic Cookery*, 1808

View from a shrubbery at Chawton House

as the year varied . . . ." Emma and Mr. Knightley walk in the longer path, taking 20 to 30 minutes to complete one circuit, making it possibly a mile or so in total length. Mr. Woodhouse, feeble and slow, takes a mere 15 minutes to complete three circuits of the shorter walk, as he calls it, "my three turns—my winter walk," so the smaller walk at Hartfield must necessarily be quite short and close to the house. The shrubberies at Cleveland, the Palmers' estate in *Sense and Sensibility*, are more extensive. Marianne Dashwood wanders

"Gravel-walks are formed for *use;*— chiefly for the convenience and comfort of the more tender sex, in this our cool and humid climate." — *The Monthly Review*, 1794

> through the winding shrubberies, now just beginning to be in beauty, to gain a distant eminence, where, from its Grecian temple, her eye, wandering over a wide tract of country to the south east, could fondly rest on the farthest ridge of hills in the horizon. . . .

In the Garden with Jane Austen

And when she is imprudent enough to take two twilight walks "not merely on the dry gravel of the shrubbery, but all over the grounds, and especially in the most distant parts of them, where there was something more of wildness than in the rest, where the trees were the oldest, and the grass was the longest and wettest," she acquires an illness that nearly kills her.

Some garden designers recommended paths wide enough to accommodate at least three walkers abreast. In *Pride and Prejudice* the paths at Mr. Bingley's estate, Netherfield, are exactly that wide. Elizabeth Bennet finds that "the path just admitted three," allowing only Mr. Darcy, Miss Bingley, and Mrs. Hurst to walk together. Rather than tag along, Elizabeth chooses to ramble off by herself. It was considered desirable that paths should lead to a particular destination, such as an outbuilding (preferably decorative) or to separate gardens:

Walking dress for 1812, from Ackermann's Repository of Arts

> In extensive shrubberies, each walk should lead to some particular Object; to the orchard, kitchen garden, botanical borders, green-house, dairy, ice-house, mushroom-hut, aviary, poultry-yard, or stables. The intention of the plantation should seem to be, to conduct the walker in the most agreeable manner to each outlet and building of utility or pleasure.
> — *Sylva Florifera: The Shrubbery*, 1823

Shrubberies could be planted chiefly on one side of the pathway, an "open shrubbery," or on both, a "closed shrubbery," but esthetically an open walk was considered more desirable, as it allowed attractive views of the estate to be seen. In *Sense and Sensibility*, the Palmers' shrubbery at Cleveland is an open shrubbery. The plants, shrubs (especially flowering shrubs), and trees of a shrubbery were planted in the manner of a flower border, by height, with the flowers in front, the bushes in the middle, and the trees in the back. On the open side of the path would be planted a few trees, spaced to give shade to the walkers, but far enough apart from each other to keep the view open. Garden books advised planting with an eye to the contrasting shades of green of the bushes, and to the succession of bloom of the shrubs and flowers. Owners sometimes planted bushes, trees, and flowers at regularly spaced intervals, but this was not considered to be in the best of taste, looking, said the author of *Sylva Florifera*, like "beaux and belles standing up for a quadrille or country dance." Groups of shrubs, for "a mass of color," were preferable.

Love in the Shrubbery

In *Emma*, the garden is nearly the only place for the heroine to get away from her father, an elderly man whose emotional and physical needs demand her constant attention:

> Emma resolved to be out of doors as soon as possible. Never had the exquisite sight, smell, sensation of nature, tranquil, warm, and brilliant after a storm, been more attractive to her. She longed for the serenity they might gradually introduce; and on Mr. Perry's coming in soon after dinner, with a disengaged hour to give her father, . . . she lost no time in hurrying into the shrubbery.—There, with spirits freshened, and thoughts a little relieved, she had taken a few turns . . . .

Distressed heroines such as Emma may have found rest and refuge in the garden, but the pleasure grounds of a country estate, filled with winding paths and secret nooks, formed perfect settings for lovers as well. In Jane Austen's time, unmarried young women and men were not supposed to be left alone together, which rather limited young lovers' abilities to do more than engage in publicly acceptable conversation and exchange tender glances. But opportunities to converse and cuddle, so scarce indoors, could easily be found in the garden—under the guise of the socially acceptable walk. Jane Austen knew well how necessary to love privacy was.

Jane Bennet and Bingley walk alone in the shrubbery in *Pride and Prejudice*, Fanny Price and Edmund Bertram fall in love "wandering about and sitting under trees . . . all the summer evenings" at Mansfield Park, and, most romantically, Darcy proposes for the second, successful time, to Elizabeth Bennet as they walk from the Bennet's estate to a neighboring house. Indeed, most of the proposal scenes in the novels take place out of doors, understandably. Who except Mr. Collins would want to propose in front of Mrs. Bennet?

[S]he saw Mr. Knightley passing through the garden door, and coming towards her. . . . "My dearest Emma," said he, ". . . tell me at once. Say 'No,' if it is to be said." She could really say nothing.— "You are silent," he cried, with great animation; "absolutely silent! at present I ask no more."
— *Emma*

In the Garden with Jane Austen

A rustic path and bridge at The Leasowes, Halesowen

"A prettyish kind of a little wilderness"

In *Sense and Sensibility*, the Palmers' estate, Cleveland, boasts not only a shrubbery, but also a "closer wood walk," that is, a path through a grove of trees carefully chosen and arranged to convey the sense to walkers of wandering through a natural forest. At Northanger Abbey, General Tilney possesses a "thick grove of old Scotch firs," through which a "narrow winding path" runs in a pleasingly melancholy fashion, much to heroine Catherine Morland's delight. At Longbourn, the Bennets' estate in *Pride and Prejudice*, there is a walk that runs through a little copse wood, which Darcy's snobbish aunt, Lady Catherine de Bourgh, calls "a prettyish kind of a little wilderness." Mr. Darcy has arranged paths at Pemberley through his very extensive woods, "some of the finest woods in the country," leading along the trout stream and up to "higher grounds; whence, in spots where the opening of the trees gave the eye power to wander, were many charming views of the valley, the opposite hills, with the long range of woods overspreading many, and occasionally part of the stream."

   Garden designers thought it important to match the character of the path, the seats, and the plants with the wilder character of the wood walk. Consequently, probably fewer flowers would have been found in a "wilderness" wood walk than in a shrubbery, though those considered appropriate to woodlands such as violets, primroses, and snowdrops might be allowed to grow scattered here and there in a natural fashion. Paths, of dirt or turf rather than gravel, ran only in approved serpentine curves. Seats placed at strategic intervals along the paths for resting and viewing the scenery were as rustic as possible, often merely sawn stumps or benches made of roughly joined tree limbs. Any structures encountered along the path were to be suitably simple and rustic as well, and Darcy's bridge across the stream at Pemberley is in the best of taste:

> ... [T]hey pursued the accustomed circuit; which brought them again, after some time, in a descent among hanging woods, to the edge of the water, and one of its narrowest parts. They crossed it by a simple bridge, in character with the general air of the scene; it was a spot less adorned than any they had yet visited . . . .

The direction of the walk ought to be guided by the points of view to which it leads, and the nature of the ground it passes over: it ought to be made subservient to the natural impediments—the Ground, Wood, and Water—which fall in its way, without appearing to have any direction of its own. It can seldom, with propriety, run any distance, in a straight line; a thing which rarely occurs in a natural walk.
— *On Planting and Rural Ornament,* 1803

Temples, Gothic Seats, Grottoes, and Hermitages

Gothic novels and romantic poetry greatly influenced the decorative structures built in eighteenth- and early nineteenth-century pleasure grounds. Nature, no longer tamed in the garden, inspired a wide range of emotions, people believed, from the soothing to the terrifying, and the way a garden or a path was constructed and decorated could assist in inspiring those emotions. Owners earlier in the eighteenth century often laid out a walk in a planned circuit, with the path leading from one carefully chosen viewpoint or object to another. At each stop would be placed a seat, an urn, or a bust with a thoughtful inscription (preferably in Latin), or perhaps a temple or gothic structure. Famous gardens, such as William Shenstone's The Leasowes, even had printed guides that led the walker from one point to another, pointing out the significance of each object or view and the appropriate associated emotion to be felt. Classically trained gentlemen put great emphasis on the "propriety" of the placement of the objects. An urn with a verse on the mortality of man, for example, required a quiet, melancholy location, but the bust of a great hero required matching grandeur.

By Jane Austen's time, simpler, more natural walks were in fashion, though many estates still had their temples, hermitages, grottoes, and gothic seats, which were useful for resting, reading, and taking tea. Godmersham, Jane brother Edward's estate in Kent, had two classical temples (which still stand) in its grounds, as well as a gothic seat. Jane's young nieces Fanny and Anna liked to read in the seat, which was probably a small covered structure with seats inside, rustic in design, perhaps with partially open sides and a thatched roof. Fanny wrote in her diary

William Shenstone's The Leasowes

The Leasowes

Halesowen, West Midlands
Tel: +44 (0)1384 814642
dudley.gov.uk

William Shenstone's The Leasowes is now a 140-acre park and nature reserve. Much of the original design has been lost or destroyed over the years, but an extensive restoration project is underway. The Leasowes is listed as a Grade I property on the English Heritage "Register of Parks and Gardens of Special Historic Interest in England."

for July 2, 1805: "Anna and I read romances in the Gothic seat."

The Bennets in *Pride and Prejudice* have a hermitage in their wilderness walk. Mrs. Bennet wants to show it off to the visiting Lady Catherine de Bourgh: "Go, my dear," she cries, "and show her ladyship about the different walks. I think she will be pleased with the hermitage." A hermitage, meant to resemble the hut of a religious recluse and to inspire melancholy associations, ought properly to be located in a secluded wooded area, so the Bennets hermitage is sited correctly, though perhaps too close to the house for the best taste.

Estate owners occasionally advertised for hermits to fill their hermitages. Employers asked such men to let their hair and fingernails grow, wear simple clothing, live in the hermitage, and interact with any passing visitors in the character of the religious ascetic. Some contracts promised large payments at the end of specified terms, because it was so hard to keep a good hermit. Eventually, the notion of hiring a hermit was considered so ridiculous that a play called *The London Hermit* lampooned it, and indeed it's hard to imagine even Mrs. Bennet going so far.

Gilbert White's House

Very near Chawton, at Selborne, lived the great naturalist and gardener Gilbert White (1720-1793), author of the world-famous *Natural History of Selborne*. The Austens were on visiting terms with the family of one of his nephews, John White, who lived in Selborne for a time after his uncle's death. "I hear that Dr White means to call on me before he leaves the Country," Jane wrote in 1816.

Gilbert White delighted in expanding and decorating his garden. He experimented with different growing methods, meticulously recording his findings, and is now considered the father of modern scientific recording.

White's beautifully restored house is now a museum of his life and work. The gardens faithfully

A Hermit in the Garden

Pere. Read that paper.

Tom P. Paper! *(reads the advertisement)* "A liberal offer.—Wanted a person to sit dressed as a hermit in the hermitage of very capital gardens: on condition of his attendance for five years, he will be entitled to a gratuity of one thousand pounds, and three hundred a year for the remainder of his life. . . . Eh! what's all this about? Hermit!

Pere. Tom, don't you think sitting in the hermitage preferable to a coop in the King's Bench. Suppose you apply for this. . . .

Tom P. Be independent of uncle— dress'd up in a gown and long beard, dam'me, I'll be a fine old bald-headed buck—besides the change in my person, if the marshal should send constables down here after me—the very thing!

—John O'Keeffe, *The London Hermit*, 1798

The garden at Gilbert White's House

Gilbert White's House

The Wakes, High Street
Selborne, Hampshire
Tel: +44 (0)1420 511275
gilbertwhiteshouse.org.uk

Gilbert White's house is located in the charming Hampshire village of Selborne, less than five miles from Jane Austen's House Museum at Chawton. The garden and grounds (over 20 acres), which were documented in detail by White, have been restored in large part to their eighteenth-century form. Plants and flowers of his time are displayed in the gardens, including the "Six Quarters" garden, a wildflower garden, an herb garden, and a vegetable garden. The interior of the house itself has been restored according to descriptions in White's correspondence. Displays include the original manuscript of his book. The tea parlour serves refreshments, including some based on eighteenth-century recipes.

The conservatory at Stoneleigh Abbey

Stoneleigh Abbey

Kenilworth, Warwickshire
Tel: +44 (0)1926 858535
stoneleighabbey.org

The nine beautifully restored grand state rooms at Stoneleigh Abbey are open for tours, as are the restored stables and the grounds. Humphry Repton designed the lovely pleasure grounds and park, with changes that included widening the River Avon, three years after Jane Austen's visit. Flower gardens in the front of the house have been restored to the appearance of that time. The Jane Austen Tour covers the history of Jane's visit and the Leigh family association with the Abbey (Mrs. Austen was born a Leigh). One of the ornate rooms shown includes the pleasant, sunny room where Mrs. Austen, Cassandra, and Jane sat looking out over the river as they ate breakfast or wrote letters.

In the Garden with Jane Austen

represent the gardens planted by White during his residence there, with ongoing research continuing to refine and improve the accuracy of the re-creation. Visitors may follow several walks of various lengths through the floral and herb gardens, the kitchen gardens, or out past the ha-ha to the orchard and beyond.

Stoneleigh Abbey

When the great estate of Stoneleigh Abbey passed to Thomas Leigh, a cousin of Mrs. Austen, in 1806 while Mrs. Austen, Cassandra, and Jane were visiting him, he and his guests set off to Warwickshire to view his inheritance. The Abbey, converted (as was the fictional Northanger Abbey) to a private house when Henry VIII dissolved the monasteries of England, was a large, handsome house with extensive pleasure grounds. On arriving, Mrs. Austen wrote to her daughter-in-law about the estate, pleased with the house and the grounds, but, predictably, fascinated most by the huge kitchen garden:

'Engaged by the river'

> [H]ere we all found ourselves on Tuesday . . . everything is very grand & very fine & very large. The house is larger than I could have supposed. . . . I expected to find everything about the place very fine and all that, but I had no idea of its being so beautiful. . . . The Avon runs near the house amidst green meadows bounded by large and beautiful woods, full of delightful walks. . . .
>
> We walk a great deal, for the woods are impenetrable to the sun even in the middle of an August day. I do not fail to spend some time every day in the kitchen garden where the quantities of small fruits exceed anything you can form an idea of. This large family with the assistance of a great many blackbirds and thrushes cannot prevent its rotting on the trees. The garden contains 5 acres and a half. The ponds supply excellent fish, the park excellent venison; there is also great plenty of pigeons, rabbits, & all sort of poultry, a delightful dairy where is made butter, good Warwickshire cheese & cream ditto.

— Letter from Mrs. Austen to Mary Austen, 13 August 1806

Stoneleigh Abbey, with its beautiful gardens, noble bridge, romantic deer park, splendid apartments, spacious chapel, &c, &c. is most delightfully situated . . . surrounded by towering and spreading woods, and having all the concomitants of water, rock and meadow, that are generally considered necessary to the perfection of landscape, and a ride hither, whether he be fortunate enough to gain access to the interior of the magnificent mansion or not, will well repay the attention of the visitor.

— *The Visitor's New Guide to the Spa of Leamington Priors, And its Vicinity*, 1818

The Abbey, with its impressive architecture and beautiful grounds, could serve as the model for many of the larger estates in Jane Austen's novels, and perhaps it did. The description of the chapel at Sotherton Court in *Mansfield Park*, for example, matches the chapel at Stoneleigh very closely.

The Estate Gardener

All the great estates required gardeners, sometimes many, to maintain their pleasure grounds and gardens. In addition to a kitchen garden to supply vegetables and fruit for the family, most large estates had vast manicured lawns, wood walks, extensively planted shrubberies, flower beds, and conservatories and hothouses, all of which demanded intensive labor. The taste and finances of the owner dictated the extent and style of his gardens. Jane Austen knew about the effort, money, and servants necessary to manage these large gardens from visiting her brother's estates, and her novels show that. General Tilney, ambitious and rich, has astonishingly large kitchen gardens at Northanger Abbey:

Iris

> The kitchen garden was to be next admired, and he led the way to it across a small portion of the park. The number of acres contained in this garden was such as Catherine could not listen to without dismay, being more than double the extent of all Mr. Allen's, as well her father's, including church yard and orchard. The walls seemed countless in number, endless in length; a village of hot-houses seemed to arise among them, and a whole parish to be at work within the enclosure. The general was flattered by her looks of surprise, which told him . . . that she had never seen any gardens at all equal to them before; and he then modestly owned that, "without any ambition of that sort himself—without any solicitude about it—he did believe them to be unrivalled in the kingdom."

A small estate needed perhaps one gardener with an assistant or two under him, but the great estates had many: a head gardener, who was an important personage in his own right, and several under-gardeners beneath him. Blenheim Palace had 100 outdoor laborers, 30 of whom worked in the pleasure grounds. The best gardeners came from Scotland, people thought, and indeed in *Persuasion* Sir Walter Elliot, one of Jane Austen's most snobbish landowners, employs a gardener named Mackenzie.

Cottesbrook Hall

Northampton, Northamptonshire
Tel: +44 (0)1604 505808
cottesbrookehall.co.uk

Thought by some people to be Jane Austen's inspiration for *Mansfield Park*, Cottesbrooke Hall is a striking example of Queen Anne architecture. Set in magnificent parkland, it has extensive, beautiful gardens, which won the Historic Houses Association/Christie's "Garden of the Year" Award in 2000.

The Vyne

Sherborne St John, Basingstoke,
Hampshire
Tel: +44 (0)1256 883858
nationaltrust.org.uk

The Vyne, a splendid red brick Tudor house, was owned by the Chutes, acquaintances of the Austen family. There is no positive proof that Jane Austen herself ever visited The Vyne, but we know that other members of her family were frequent guests. The house is set in extensive parkland and features beautiful gardens that include an eighteenth-century walled garden, a wild garden, an Edwardian garden, herbaceous borders, and a summerhouse dating from about 1635, possibly one of the earliest in England.

The Walled Garden at Goodnestone Park, Kent

Goodnestone Park

Goodnestone, Kent
Tel: +44 (0)1304 840107
goodnestoneparkgardens.co.uk

Goodnestone Park, a charming brick house dating to 1704, was well known to Jane Austen. Her brother Edward married Elizabeth Bridges, the daughter of the house, and Jane visited Goodnestone regularly. The 15 acres of lovely gardens include the famous Walled Garden, an old-fashioned rose garden, a summer garden, a kitchen garden, an alpine garden, and an ornamental greenhouse.

Kitchen Gardens, Conservatories, and Hothouses

Owners of country estates depended greatly on their own gardens to supply food for themselves and their servants, devoting substantial amounts of their property for that purpose. In addition to orchards, most estates contained kitchen gardens, often walled off from the rest of the grounds for security from human and animal predators, and to provide a sheltered growing environment. The kitchen gardens of large houses commonly covered several acres; General Tilney's kitchen gardens, though very extensive, would not have been considered unreasonable for a house the size of Northanger Abbey. In addition to the vegetables and smaller fruits grown in the central portion of kitchen gardens, fruit trees were trained up the walls, which provided shelter, reflected warmth, and hastened the harvest. An early harvest, even a year-round harvest, formed a major part of the duties of estate gardeners. Having a great deal of money enabled landowners such as Mr. Darcy to enjoy fruits and flowers grown out of season. When Elizabeth Bennet visits Pemberley in July, Miss Darcy offers refreshments:

Greenhouse Grapes

Greenhouse Pineapple

> The next variation which their visit afforded was produced by the entrance of servants with cold meat, cake, and a variety of all the finest fruits in season . . . . There was now employment for the whole party—for though they could not all talk, they could all eat; and the beautiful pyramids of grapes, nectarines, and peaches soon collected them round the table.

Though some varieties of nectarines and peaches ripen early, they were generally grown under glass; ripe grapes in July are almost certainly the product of a greenhouse.

Glassed-in greenhouses, hothouses, and conservatories all served the purpose of keeping Britain's wet, cold winters at bay. Conservatories and greenhouses provided shelter for plants and trees that required only some protection from the weather; stoves and hot air flues heated hothouses to protect tender and exotic plants and to force fruits and flowers out of season. Among General Tilney's "village of hot-houses" at Northanger Abbey is a pinery, a special hothouse for raising pineapples, difficult and expensive to grow, and consequently a great luxury. When General Tilney mentions that his pinery "had yielded only one hundred" pineapples in the last year, he is really boasting of his wealth: pineapples in Jane Austen's day sold for a guinea or more apiece, perhaps as much as $100 (£50) in today's money.

Some conservatories and greenhouses were elegant structures, designed to house the estate owners' special plants, and to provide a pleasant place to wander in inclement weather. Often placed near the house or even connecting with it, they blurred the line between the indoors and out. They even housed entertainments, such as at the ball Jane Austen attended at the Bigg-Withers' house, Manydown (where some years later Jane accepted, then turned down, Harris Bigg-Wither's marriage proposal):

Snapdragon

> I danced twice with Warren last night, and once with Mr. Charles Watkins, and, to my inexpressible astonishment, I entirely escaped John Lyford. I was forced to fight hard for it, however. We had a very good supper, and the greenhouse was illuminated in a very elegant manner.
> — Letter from Jane Austen to Cassandra, 9 January 1796

Gentry in the Garden

Many ladies and gentlemen took a personal interest in gardening. For some, such as Jane Austen's mother, it provided both enjoyment and exercise. Her granddaughter later wrote of her:

Nigella

> She found plenty of occupation for herself in gardening and needlework. The former was, with her, no idle pastime, no mere cutting of roses and tying up of flowers. She dug up her own potatoes, and I have no doubt she planted them, for the kitchen garden was as much her delight as the flower borders, and I have heard my mother say that when at work, she wore a green round frock like a day-labourer's.

In *Pride and Prejudice*, the sycophantic Mr. Collins enjoys working in his garden, "one of his most respectable pleasures," with the added benefit that it keeps him out of his long-suffering wife's hair. Mrs. Grant in *Mansfield Park* and Anne Elliot's arrogant sister, Elizabeth, in *Persuasion* both have collections of special plants, and though it is difficult to say whether they do any of the work themselves, one guesses that Elizabeth, at least, merely directs her gardener. Fanny Price (who keeps geraniums in her little room) loves a garden, though when she works in one, cutting roses

Remains of a greenhouse at Chawton House

Trimmed box hedges separate the areas of flowers and fruit in the kitchen garden at Chawton House.

in the flower garden at Mansfield Park, it's because her domineering aunt, Mrs. Norris, orders her to. The lethargic Lady Bertram's notion of gardening is to watch:

> "Yes, indeed, Edmund, . . . I was out above an hour. I sat three quarters of an hour in the flower garden, while Fanny cut the roses; and very pleasant it was, I assure you, but very hot. It was shady enough in the alcove, but I declare I quite dreaded the coming home again."
>
> "Fanny has been cutting roses, has she?"
>
> "Yes, and I am afraid they will be the last this year. Poor thing! She found it hot enough; but they were so full blown that one could not wait. . . . [T]he heat

In the Garden with Jane Austen

Recipes for Mrs. Norris's Dried Roses

Fine scented Wash-ball.
TAKE of the best White Soap, half a pound, and shave it into thin slices with a knife; then take two ounces and a half of Florentine Orrice, three quarters of an ounce of Calamus Aromaticus, and: the same quantity of Elder Flowers; of Cloves, and dried Rose Leaves, each half an ounce; Coriander-seed's, Lavender, and Bay Leaves, of each a drachm, with three-drachms of Storax. Reduce the whole to fine powder, which knead into a Paste with, the Soap; adding a few grains of Musk or Ambergrise. When you make this Paste into Wash-balls, soften it with a little Oil of Almonds to render the composition more lenient. Too much, cannot be said in favour of this Wash-ball, with regard to its cleansing and cosmetic property.

Bags to scent Linen.
TAKE Rose Leaves dried in the shade, Cloves beat to a gross powder, and Mace scraped; mix them together, and put the composition into little bags.
— *The Toilet of Flora*, 1779

was enough to kill anybody. It was as much as I could bear myself. Sitting and calling to Pug, and trying to keep him from the flower beds, was almost too much for me."

The acquisitive Mrs. Norris naturally intends the roses for use at her own cottage and makes Fanny deliver them there, regardless of the heat of the day.

Royal Pavilion, Brighton

"The Garden is the best in the Town"
CITY GARDENS

A gravel roller at the Georgian Garden in Bath

> *[T]he garden is quite a love. . . . I live in [the] room downstairs, it is particularly pleasant, from opening upon the garden. I go & refresh myself every now & then, and then come back to Solitary Coolness.*
>
> — Letter from Jane Austen to Cassandra, 23 August 1814

Narrow green oases of calm and tranquility, town gardens were a saving consolation in the smoky, noisy cities of Jane Austen's day. Exciting though city life could be, it nevertheless meant trading pleasant, open gardens for confined, airless spaces. In their town gardens, Jane and her heroines could find not only greenery and flowers, but rest, solace, and inspiration.

Refreshment in the Garden

Jane Austen liked a visit now and then to Bath or London. As a young woman, she had appreciated short holidays in Bath and London; like the giddy Catherine Morland who visits

Bath in *Northanger Abbey*, she attended plays, concerts, and dancing assemblies, shopped and went sightseeing, and generally enjoyed herself very much. But she agreed with Isabella Thorpe in *Northanger Abbey*, that "though it is vastly well to be here for a few weeks, we would not live here for millions."

Judging by her novels and letters, Jane Austen disliked living in cities, the gloomy gray rains splashing on the dirty pavements in winter and the "white glare" reflecting off the hard stone and brick walls in summer. She missed her country freedom, "of wandering from place to place in free and luxurious solitude" (*Sense and Sensibility*). Forced by her father's retirement to leave her beloved childhood home in the pleasant, wildflower-filled country of Steventon, Hampshire, she lived in Bath for five years, and she couldn't wait to get out. Later she wrote, "It will be two years tomorrow since we left Bath . . . with what happy feelings of Escape!"

What compensations could Jane possibly have found in Bath for the loss of the Austens' large country parsonage home, surrounded as it was by flower gardens, shady trees, and leafy country walks? She made do with a little refuge: the town garden. Behind most of the newer houses of her time were long, narrow, walled gardens, hidden from the streets, green havens in a hard, stone city. There wasn't much space in them—room, perhaps, for a gravel walk, a few small trees and shrubs, and a seat or two, but it was enough: a place to walk, to think, to sit and be refreshed.

But Does It Have a Garden?

The Austens considered many properties, but all had some fault: too small, too damp, too hot, too expensive. Some areas were more fashionable (and more expensive) than others, and balancing fashion, comfort, and price could be tricky. Jane and Cassandra originally hoped for Laura Place (an up-market location away from the main part of Bath, and guaranteed to have a nice garden), but Mrs. Austen hoped to live in Queen Square: "I join with you in wishing for the Environs of Laura place," Jane wrote to Cassandra in January 1801, "but do not venture to expect it.—My Mother hankers after the Square [Queen] dreadfully." Mr. Austen was apparently first concerned only with expense, though he adjusted his ideas as the search for housing went on.

Moving from the country meant inevitable losses—gone was the large garden in which the Austens had grown not only flowers but also much of their food, and where Cassandra had kept bees. Jane teased her about it: "In what part of Bath do you mean to place your Bees?— We are afraid of the South Parade's being too hot." Mrs. Austen, an avid gardener, no doubt wished for a house with a pleasant garden in back to compensate for the loss of their country garden, and Jane, too, wished for a little greenery when she speculated on possible addresses: "It would be very pleasant to be near Sydney Gardens!—we might go into the Labyrinth every day." Ultimately the Austens did settle on No. 4 Sydney Place, directly across the street from Sydney Gardens. Not only was Jane able to go walking there, but No. 4 also boasted a town garden in back.

The Georgian Garden, Bath

Georgian Garden

No. 4, The Circus, Bath
bathnes.co.uk, under "Environment
& Planning," "Parks & Open
Spaces," "Parks, Grounds &
Public Open Spaces"

The entrance to the Georgian Garden is from the
Gravel Walk in Royal Victoria Park, between Royal
Crescent and Queen Square.

A Georgian Garden in Bath

The Austens' main house in Bath, No. 4 Sydney Place, where they lived from 1801 to 1805, is not currently open to the public except by special arrangement, but a similar garden, restored to its delightful late-eighteenth-century appearance, is. In 1984 the Bath Preservation Trust decided to re-create the garden of No. 4, The Circus (the headquarters of the Bath Museums Service) as an example of a Georgian-style town garden. Fortunately, the Bath Archaeological Trust suggested excavating the site before any re-creations were carried out. Under a layer of fill, archaeologists found the original, circa 1760-70 formal garden less than 16 inches (0.4 meters) below the surface, complete with paths, flower beds, and even the original gravel still in place. They carefully scraped away the later fill, exposing the garden, and planted it with shrubs and flowers appropriate to the period. Trellises, placed where the originals once stood, clipped box hedges, and the sorts of specimen plants and double flowers beloved by gardeners of the time all combine to make a charming vision of a Georgian Bath garden. It's easy to imagine Jane Austen's characters walking in this calm scene, perhaps Anne Elliot, taking refuge from the noisy Bath she and Jane Austen disliked so much: "the dash of . . . carriages, the heavy rumble of carts and drays, the bawling of newspapermen, muffin men and milkmen, and the ceaseless clink of pattens."

Snowdrop

"A lofty dignified situation"

Like the Austens themselves, Jane Austen's characters are very concerned about where to live, but the houses they choose tell us more about their social status and aspirations than their interest in a town garden. Surely Anne Elliot, the gentle heroine of *Persuasion*, wishes for a house with a pleasant garden in which she could escape her rather unpleasant family, but her father, the comically arrogant Sir Walter Elliot, thinks only of his social status. The readers of the time would have known which were the best addresses, which were the middle sorts, and which addresses Sir Walter would think were downright vulgar and socially beyond the pale. He is keenly aware of these distinctions and is anxious to know whether some acquaintances "were likely to be situated in such a part of Bath as it might suit Miss Elliot and himself to visit in." In Jane Austen's earlier work *Northanger Abbey* (written around 1798-99), the main town area is still ultra-fashionable, though the properties there generally had only small gardens at best. The Thorpes live in Edgar's Buildings in George Street, status-conscious General Tilney lives in Milsom Street, and when Jane and her mother stayed with Jane's rich brother, Edward, at No. 13 Queen Square in 1799, they were staying at one of Bath's best addresses.

The development of new, fashionable crescents such as the Circus and the Royal Crescent on the edges of Bath gradually demoted formerly upper-end addresses: by the time Jane Austen began writing *Persuasion* in 1815, perceptions of the main part of town were beginning to change. The Musgrove daughters, badgering their father to take them to Bath, cry, "Remember, papa, if we do go, we must be in a good situation—none of your Queen-squares for us!" Sir Walter Elliot, who is nothing if not protective of his rank and dignity, chooses Camden Place: "Sir Walter had taken a very good house in Camden Place, a lofty dignified situation, such as becomes a man of consequence" and the Elliots' grand cousin, the Dowager Viscountess Dalrymple, "had taken a house, for three months, in Laura Place, and would be living in style." All of these new developments featured attractive gardens, often prominently advertised to prospective renters and buyers. Developers were careful to preserve green spaces, areas where residents could stroll and enjoy a respite from town life. Jane Austen often enjoyed walking near one of the finest of these developments, the Royal Crescent.

The Royal Crescent

Built between 1767 and 1775 by John Wood the Younger, the Royal Crescent was the first such curved terrace in Great Britain. Instantly fashionable, the 30 houses in the Crescent, some of the more expensive houses in Bath, were snapped up by the upper crust of society. The Duke of York, the second son of George III, lived at No. 16, which boasted a huge rear garden complete with a coach house and stables large enough for 16 horses. No. 16, combined with No. 15, is now the site of The Royal Crescent Hotel. Jane Austen's aunt and uncle, the Coopers, lived for a time at No. 12, which is now divided into flats, as are most of the houses in the Crescent. No. 1 lacks a garden, but the interior has been restored to Georgian splendor and is now a museum open to the public.

The Crescent, with its imposing colonnaded facade, commands beautiful views of Bath over what is now Victoria Park. In front is the original lawn, separated from the park below by a "ha-ha," a sunken fence which formerly separated the field below from the lawn and kept any roving livestock from straying into the manicured areas. Recent archaeological excavations uncovered an unexpectedly ancient aspect to the Crescent: the remains of a Roman road, sweeping uphill through the lawn and running right under the Coopers' house at No. 12.

The area in front of the Royal Crescent was a fashionable promenade in Jane Austen's day, *de rigeur* for those who wanted to see and be seen. In *Northanger Abbey*, she tells us that "a fine Sunday in Bath empties every house of its inhabitants, and all the world appears on such an occasion to walk about and tell their acquaintance what a charming day it is." Jane often walked there herself on Sundays to stroll and talk with her friends and acquaintances. In 1801 she wrote to Cassandra: "On Sunday we went to church twice, and after evening service walked a little in the Crescent fields, but found it too cold to stay long," and in 1805: "Miss Irvine invited us, when I met her in the Crescent, to drink tea with them . . . . We did not walk long in the Crescent . . . . It was hot and not crowded enough; so we went into the field." That field is now Victoria Park.

Gardening in Town

Gardening in towns and cities had its own particular difficulties, bad air, bad water, and bad soil chief among them. Lack of space was also a major concern. Elizabeth Elliot in *Persuasion* seems

The gardens at The Royal Crescent Hotel

The Royal Crescent Hotel

16 Royal Crescent, Bath
Tel: +44 (0)1225 823333
Free phone: 0800 980 0987
U.S. toll free phone: 1 888 295 4710
royalcrescent.co.uk

The Royal Crescent Hotel occupies the two central buildings of the Royal Crescent. The gardens behind the two houses and parts of several others have been thrown together to create a beautiful, secluded tea garden. The buildings behind the hotel, including the former coach houses, now contain a spa and a restaurant and bar. The restaurant is open daily for tea, lunch, and dinner. The gardens are open to hotel and restaurant guests.

The Royal Crescent, Bath

No. 1 Royal Crescent Museum

No. 1 Royal Crescent, Bath
Tel: +44 (0)1225 428126
bath-preservation-trust.org.uk

The No. 1 Royal Crescent Museum is a grand townhouse run by the Bath Preservation Trust, which has restored the house to its former eighteenth-century elegance. The décor and furnishings present an authentic re-creation of how the house might have appeared in Jane Austen's time.

to take quite an interest in gardening, one of the best things we know about her (though we can bet she never actually soils her own aristocratic fingers in garden dirt), yet there would have been relatively few opportunities for her to indulge her interests in Bath. Town gardens, even the biggest, were necessarily little, and were usually planted in the old geometric style, as being more appropriate to a small space. Once the gravel walks, trees, and shrubs were laid out, and a few flowers chosen, not much remained to do. Still, where they had space, city dwellers were driven to try.

> Although it is true that near London plants in general will not thrive so well as in purer air . . . yet such persons as are condemned to a town life will do well to obtain whatever substitute for a garden may be in their power.
> — *Flora Domestica*, 1823

Gardening advice books counseled bringing in new soil to replace the rubble that underlay most city gardens, and printed lists of trees and flowers that would "bear the Smoak of the Town." Lime (linden) trees were recommended, as they grew "where other trees will not grow."

Geranium psilostemon

Stocks, pinks, carnations, geraniums, lilies of the valley, wallflowers, and mignonettes were all considered hardy enough to withstand life in the town garden, though certain precautions had to be taken with anything planted there. "Syringe" (squirt) their leaves with water, the experts admonished, or plants would suffocate from the accumulated soot. The soot, rising with the smoke from innumerable coal fires, was notorious. It dismayed visitors:

The air, in the mean time, is loaded with small flakes of smoke . . . a sort of flower of soot, so light as to float without falling. This black snow sticks to your clothes and linen, or lights on your face. You just feel something on your nose, or your cheek,—the finger is applied mechanically, and fixes it into a black patch!
—Louis Simond, *Journal of a Tour and Residence in Great Britain During the Years 1810 and 1811*

London Garden Squares

For those with enough money, such as Jane Austen's brother Henry, a banker, money made avoiding the smog of London easier. By the end of the eighteenth century, most of the gentry chose to live to the northwest and west of London, in elegant new terraces and squares out of reach, for the most part, of city soot. The "western environs" surrounding London exhibited, according to the 1817 tour book *Walks Through London*, "the appearance of a continual garden, with extensive nurseries of trees of various kinds; while the sides of the roads being enlivened by meadows and genteel residences of every description, the whole forms a picture of ease and happiness highly gratifying." Some of Henry Austen's houses, at Michael's Place, Sloane Street, and Hans Place, were in the Chelsea or Kensington area; when Jane visited Henry there, she spoke of walking *into* London to do her shopping.

Garden squares, in particular, were thought to have "salubrious" or healthy air, which made them and their surrounding streets particularly desirable addresses. Built around central, private gardens that were accessible only to residents of the square, they served then, as they do now, as open and uncrowded oases of green. Several of Jane Austen's richer characters live in or near squares. In *Emma*, Emma's sister Isabella lives in "airy" Brunswick Square. In *Sense and Sensibility*, rich acquaintances of the Dashwood sisters, Charlotte Palmer and her husband, live in Hanover Square, and Charlotte's mother, the good-humored and extremely wealthy Mrs. Jennings, lives in Berkeley Street right off Portman Square, one of the best squares in London.

In 1814, Jane's brother Henry, then a banker, moved to Hans Place, an elegant, elongated square to the west of his old house in Sloane Street. There was not only a lovely central garden in the square, but each of the houses also had attractive gardens behind. Henry's house, No. 23, possessed a large garden, where Henry even had a greenhouse. Jane appreciated the garden

An urn in the shrubbery of the Hans Place garden square

London Open Garden Squares Weekend

opensquares.org
londongardenstrust.org
Annually, in June

Once a year, generally in June, over 100 garden squares and other private gardens—"London's hidden treasures"—open their gates to welcome the public. Historic and modern gardens alike can be viewed, including some of London's more unusual and eccentric gardens. Some of the sites have family activities, some host tours, and many sites have refreshments available, including wine-tasting.

The Royal Pavilion at Brighton

The Royal Pavilion

Brighton
Tel: +44 (0)1273 290900
royalpavilion.org.uk

The Royal Pavilion is a former royal residence built for the Prince Regent (later George IV) as a seaside retreat. His choice of Brighton guaranteed that the resort became ultra-fashionable in Jane Austen's time. The ornate Pavilion and the extensive gardens have been restored to their former splendor. Tours of the gardens are self-guided; a special Regency Garden tour is available.

In the Garden with Jane Austen

very much during her visits to London. "[T]he Garden is quite a Love," she wrote to Cassandra. "I live in [the] room downstairs, it is particularly pleasant, from opening upon the garden. I go & refresh myself every now & then, and then come back to Solitary Coolness." Henry's house still stands in Hans Place today, though its facade was redone in Victorian brick and the garden was swept away during redevelopment. The garden in the center of the square remains, pleasant and private for the residents of what is now one of the more exclusive neighborhoods in London.

A Royal Garden

Large, magnificent gardens could be grown in towns, if the air was healthy enough, or if enough money was spent maintaining them. Carleton House, the Prince Regent's house in London, was famous for its gardens, where the prince often hosted extravagant outdoor parties. At Brighton, the popular seaside resort, the prince built himself a spectacular, highly decorated palace. The Royal Pavilion is a fantastic confection of ornately ornamented spires and domes surrounded by magnificent grounds and gardens, which were designed in the best fashionable style by Humphry Repton himself.

We are not sure if Jane Austen ever visited Brighton, but her characters definitely did. In *Mansfield Park*, the newly married Rushworths honeymoon at "gay" and "smart" Brighton "in one of the best houses there, as Mr. Rushworth's fine fortune gives them a right to be," and silly, foolish Lydia Bennet pesters her father in *Pride and Prejudice* until he allows her to visit the resort. The Pavilion is now a magnificent museum, restored to look as it did in the days of the Prince Regent. The grounds and gardens, now a public park, have also been restored to their Regency splendor.

"Flowers to blow in a House. Several sorts of bulbous roots may be placed upon bulb-glasses of water for blowing in the apartments of a house, such as hyacinths, narcissuses, jonquils, . . . &c.; the glasses for this purpose are to be had at the seed and glass-shops, being made concave at the mouth, to contain each one root, and are to be filled with soft water, and one root placed in each glass with its bottom touching the water: placing the bottles upon a shelf or chimney-piece of some light warm room, or the inside of a warm window, and if where the sun comes will be an additional advantage; . . . they will soon shoot their roots down into the water . . . and they will thus blow very agreeably, early in the spring; or may be greatly forwarded if placed in a hot-house."
— *Every Man His Own Gardener*, 1809

The narrow town garden at 25 Gay Street in Bath

"I have just learned to love a hyacinth,"

What beautiful hyacinths! I have just learnt to love a hyacinth. . . . Mrs. Allen
used to take pains, year after year, to make me like them; but I never could, till I
saw them the other day in Milsom Street.
—Catherine Morland, in *Northanger Abbey*

If a town house lacked a garden, or if that garden failed to grow, there were still ways to bring
the outdoors into the house. Plant stands and window boxes were very popular and fashionable,
and flowers were readily available from town florists to fill the elegant chinoiserie vases. But for
those who yearned for a more hands-on approach, bulb forcing was popular. Stores sold special
blown glass vases, with a wide body, a narrower neck, and a wide cup at the top for a bulb.

The Job Gardener

Only the very grandest of the city and town residences employed a full-time gardener. Most
gardening was done on a piecemeal basis, either contracted out to local nurseries who engaged
to fill the gardens with plants, maintain them, and replace the plants if they died, or by job
gardeners, who might care for many small properties at once. The Austen women hired
just such a man when they moved to the southern coastal city of Southampton and had the
garden at their new house refurbished. In fact, they hired two, an initial gardener and then
his replacement. Jane wrote to Cassandra about them in 1807: "Our Garden is putting in
order, by a Man who bears a remarkably good Character, has a very fine complexion & asks
something less than the first." Good character was important in a gardener. Garden plants and

fruits were often quite valuable, and as such were irresistible magnets for thieves. Once plucked or dug up, one fruit or plant looked much like another and could easily be resold on the street. In garden theft court cases of the time the accused's occupation is often listed as "gardener"—a gardener-thief presumably knew the most desirable plants to steal and how best to get rid of the stolen goods. A little extra "gardening" by night could provide a job gardener with nice supplemental income, provided he didn't get caught.

Necessary Evils

Though indoor water closets were becoming increasingly common (and understandably popular) in city houses by Jane Austen's day, many town dwellers faced the same ordeal in town as in the country: the inevitable trips outdoors to the outhouse, whatever the weather. Known variously as the privy, the necessity, the necessary house, and the conveniency (and jokingly, by classically educated men, "The Temple of Cloacina," for the goddess of the sewers), the outhouse held a disagreeable but essential place in the

14 September 1785: "THOMAS FROST [a gardener] was indicted for that he on the 3d day of July, about two in the night, into a certain garden ground of, and belonging to one John Renton, unlawfully did enter, and fifty young plants, called orange trees, value 6 s. twenty stock flower roots, value 3 s. three balm of gilead roots, value 6 d. from out of the same, without the consent of the said John, then and there, unlawfully, willfully, and feloniously did pluck up, dig up, take and carry away, against the statute."

VERDICT: Guilty.

PUNISHMENT: Whipped, and imprisoned one month in Newgate.

— The Proceedings of the Old Bailey for 1785

town garden. Small areas behind small city houses often had room for little else besides the privy, but even the grandest town houses had them. Owners generally placed them at the end of the garden farthest from the house and did their best to disguise them. Small, common outhouses might be made only of wood, perhaps not even painted, but the stylish owners of great town houses constructed their grander privies of brick or stone, often in impressive architectural styles—just one more ornament in an elegant garden. Garden books advised screening them with plants in front, and letting fragrant vining flowers grow over them, one assumes to help mask odors. Paths to the privy were to be circular, so that it would not be obvious to the casual observer what the stroller's purpose was in choosing that particular path. In Lady Falmouth's London garden, the celebrated gardener Joseph Spence proposed the outhouse as one of a pair of two six-foot-square structures at the far end of the garden. One structure was to be "A Little Study," the other the "Conveniency." They were to have "two trees with honey-suckles before . . . to conceal them fro[m] ye East-view" [the view from the house]. Large, ornate, covered by vines and trees, and visited by ladies in silk dresses they might be, but there they were: necessary evils.

"The rooms were dressed up with flowers"

The social season in London and Bath, when the most important parties, balls, and other entertainments took place, began in winter and ran until early summer. Many in the upper classes spent half the year in London. For these gentry, whose self-image was tightly wound up with their country estates, it was fashionable to pretend, at least, to hanker after the countryside.

Ladies and gentlemen, removed from their country estates and nature, compensated not only with what gardens they could manage, but also by filling the rooms and balconies of their town houses with potted plants and flowers. Window boxes full of flowers, particularly mignonette *(Reseda odorata)*, highly fragrant and masking the smells of a city, were common, as an American visitor to London noticed:

> June 6. —There has not been a drop of rain for the last six weeks; the verdure of the town gardens is destroyed. . . . The windows are, however, universally adorned with plants quite fresh and luxuriant,— the reseda particularly, which perfumes the air: this luxury is very general.
> — Louis Simond, *Journal of a Tour and Residence in Great Britain During the Years 1810 and 1811*

London was surrounded by nurseries and market gardens, just far enough out of town to escape most of the soot and unhealthy air. The Kensington area, near where Jane Austen's brother Henry had most of his houses, had relatively clean air and was famous for its nurseries and other commercial gardens. These gardens and others surrounding the city supplied the markets of London with everything its inhabitants needed in the way of fresh vegetables and fruit, as well as with trees, shrubs, and flowers for town house gardens, and flowers and potted plants for their balconies and interiors. Plants, bulbs, and flowers, both cut as nosegays and potted, could be purchased from street peddlers or at markets. Covent Garden, where Henry had his bank's offices (and briefly lived) at No. 10 Henrietta Street, was renowned for its selection.

> Perhaps more pots of mignionette are sold in and near the metropolis than of any other potted plant whatever. . . . Next to mignionette may be named stocks, pinks, sweet-pease and wall-flowers, among the hardy plants; hyacinths, among the bulbs; and geraniums and myrtles, among the exotics. Some years ago heaths and camellias were chiefly in repute; these being found difficult to keep in rooms, the public taste has changed, and the flower-grower varies his products accordingly.
> — *An Encyclopaedia of Gardening*, 1822

In the Garden with Jane Austen

Near the Pump Room in Bath. "What dreadful weather . . . ! It may not be felt in Bath, with your nice pavements . . . ." Persuasion.

The nurseries also supplied city dwellers directly, and a great deal of their business came from rentals. Householders contracted by the season for flowers and shrubs to fill their pots, or even rented preplanted window boxes and pots, which were often painted in some decorative fashion. For the ambitious host and hostess, commercial nurseries and market florists filled a more pressing need, that of decorating the reception rooms of their town houses with plants and flowers for (they hoped) glittering social events. The nurserymen and florists were pleased to take advantage of these social ambitions:

Upon the earth her Eyes she threw
The Flow'rets wild before her grew
Those Gifts by bounteous nature spread
She gather'd to procure them bread. . . .
Ere early light adorns the sky
She roves the Heath and Valley fenny
And tow'rds proud London hastes to Cry
Primroses, Primroses, Primroses,
Two Bunches a Penny.
— "Ellen," a popular sentimental eighteenth-century song, as transcribed by Jane Austen in her songbooks

All these, and other sorts of plants in pots, are also lent out by the market-florist, to decorate private or public rooms on extraordinary occasions, but especially for those midnight assemblages called routs. This is the most lucrative part of the grower's business, who generally receives half the value of the plants lent out, as many of them, and generally those of most value, are so injured by the heat as never to recover.

— *An Encyclopaedia of Gardening,* 1822

Henry and Eliza Austen held a large party while Jane was visiting their house in Sloane Street in 1811. A musical soirée with professional musicians, including a harpist and three glee singers, it was perhaps reminiscent of the musical party Elinor and Marianne Dashwood attend in *Sense and Sensibility:* "The party, like other musical parties, comprehended a great many people who had real taste for the performance, and a great many more who had none at all; and the performers themselves were, as usual, in their own estimation, and that of their immediate friends, the first private performers in England." Eliza (the dashing former Comtesse de Feuillide) worked for days ahead to prepare for the party, shopping and decorating. The rooms were decorated in the socially approved fashion with flowers, which were no doubt bought or rented for the occasion:

> Our party went off extremely well. There were many solicitudes, alarms & vexations beforehand, of course, but at last everything was quite right. The rooms were dressed up with flowers &c, & looked very pretty. . . . At $^1/2$ past 7 arrived the Musicians in two Hackney coaches, & by 8 the lordly Company began to appear. . . . Including everybody we were 66—which was considerably more than Eliza had expected, & quite enough to fill the Back Draw[in]g room, & leave a few to be scattered about in the other, & in the passage.— The Music was extremely good. . . . all the Performers gave great satisfaction by doing what they were paid for, & giving themselves no airs. . . . The house was not clear till after 12.
> — Letter from Jane Austen to Cassandra, 25 April 1811

"Flowers are very much worn"

Flowers not only decorated rooms in Jane Austen's time, they decorated the women as well. For an excursion to the opera, the theater, a ball, or for a grand private entertainment such as Eliza and Henry Austen's musical evening, no woman's ensemble was considered complete without either jewels or flowers. Etiquette books cautioned women against "a profuse display of conspicuous and shewy ornaments"; for young women, the author of the 1811 *Mirror of the Graces* urged the use of flowers, real or artificial:

> Their ornaments should hardly ever exceed the natural or imitated flowers of the most delicate tribes. The Snow-drop, Lilly of the Valley, Violet, Primrose, Myrtle, Provence Rose; these, and their resemblances, are embellishments which harmonize with their gaiety and blooming years.

In winter, such flowers, grown in hothouses, were readily available in towns and cities from the same nurserymen, florists, and market flower-sellers who provided flowers and plants for the decoration of town houses. Milliners and other shops sold artificial flowers, often finely painted to resemble real flowers.

Women wore flowers on their bonnets, pinned to their dresses, and in their hair. Jane Austen wore a flower, presumably an artificial one, in her hair to Eliza and Henry's party, and was pleased to hear later that she had been described as attractive by an attending guest:

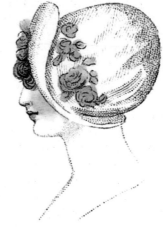

> My head dress was a Bugle band like the border to my gown, & a flower of Mrs Tilson's.—I depended upon hearing something of the Eveng from Mr W[yndham] K[natchbull] & am very well satisfied with his notice of me. "A pleasing looking young woman";—that must do;—one cannot pretend to anything better now—thankful to have it continued a few years longer!
> — Letter from Jane Austen to Cassandra, 30 April 1811

"I cannot help thinking that it is more natural to have flowers grow out of the head than fruit." Headdress for 1809.

Jane and her sister took a keen interest in fashion and its changes from season to season. Jane often wrote to Cassandra to consult her about such proposed purchases for themselves as hats, material for dresses, and lace, and, during a visit to Bath, artificial fruit and flowers.

> I saw some Gauzes in a shop in Bath Street yesterday at only 4s a yard, but they were not so good or so pretty as mine.—Flowers are very much worn, & Fruit is still more the thing.—Eliz[abeth] has a bunch of Strawberries, & I have seen Grapes, Cherries, Plumbs, & Apricots. . . . We have been to the cheap Shop, & very cheap we found it, but there are only flowers made there, no fruit—& as I could get 4 or 5 very pretty sprigs of the former for the same money which would procure only one Orleans plumb . . . I cannot decide on the fruit till I hear from you again.—Besides, I cannot help thinking that it is more natural to have flowers grow out of the head than fruit.—What do you think on that subject?
> — Letters from Jane Austen to Cassandra, 2 June & 11 June 1799

A Small Town Garden in Southampton

In January of 1805, Jane and Cassandra's father, George Austen, died. The Austen women continued to live for some time in Bath, first in a house at 25 Gay Street, which had an attractive town garden, then in lodgings in Trim Street until the summer of 1806. In October they moved to Southampton, on the southern coast, their final stop before returning to the country for good

A garden display at the Jane Austen Centre in Bath

The Jane Austen Centre

40 Gay Street, Queen Square, Bath
Tel: +44 (0) 1225 443000
janeausten.co.uk

Located near the house in Gay Street where Jane Austen once lived, this historic Georgian townhouse contains permanent exhibits highlighting Jane Austen's life in Bath and the times in which she lived. Features also include a gift shop that specializes in Jane Austen items and a Regency Tea Room that serves tea and refreshments. The Centre sponsors an annual Jane Austen Festival with lectures, Regency dances, and a costume promenade, among its many activities.

in 1809. They chose a large, pleasant house in Castle Square, so named because the owner of the Austens' new home, the eccentric Marquis of Lansdowne, lived there in a castle of a house, an oversized edifice that consumed most of the square.

Jane's nephew James often visited his grandmother and aunts and thought the situation of their house was good: "My grandmother's house had a pleasant garden, bounded on one side by the old city walls; the top of this wall was sufficiently wide to afford a pleasant walk, with an extensive view, easily accessible to ladies by steps."

Southampton was known for its healthy air. The Austens were able to grow a wide variety of trees, bushes, fruits, and flowers, almost as if they were in the country. Jane and Mrs. Austen supervised the planting in the garden while Cassandra was visiting their brother Edward, and Jane wrote to her of their plans and the recommendations of their job gardener:

These naked shoots,
Barren as lances, among which the wind
Makes wintry music, sighing as it goes
Shall put their graceful foliage on again, . . .
Laburnum, rich
In streaming gold; syringa, ivory pure;
The scentless and the scented rose; this red
And of an humbler growth, the other tall,
And throwing up into the darkest gloom
Of neighbouring cypress, or more sable yew,
Her silver globes, light as the foamy surf
That the wind severs from the broken wave
    — William Cowper, "The Task," 1785

The shrubs which border the gravel walk he says are only sweetbriar & roses, & the latter of an indifferent sort;—we mean to get a few of a better kind, therefore, & at my own particular desire he procures us some Syringas. I could not do without a Syringa, for the sake of Cowper's Line. We talk also of a Laburnum. The border under the Terrace Wall, is clearing away to receive Currants & Gooseberry Bushes, & a spot is found very proper for Raspberries. . . . We hear that we are envied our House by many people, & that the Garden is the best in the Town.
— Letters from Jane Austen to Cassandra, 8 & 21 February 1807

The syringa Jane Austen speaks of is not *Syringa vulgaris*, the lilac, but rather *Philadelphus*, mock orange, a woody shrub with highly fragrant white flowers. The Austens grew strawberries, and flowers grown from seed brought from one of Edward's estates, Godmersham. Having such a large, airy garden must have been pleasing to the Austens following their years in Bath. The site where the house, its garden, and the castle stood has been redeveloped, but portions of the old city wall can still be seen.

Jane Austen's beloved syringa (Mock Orange) at Sydney Gardens, Bath

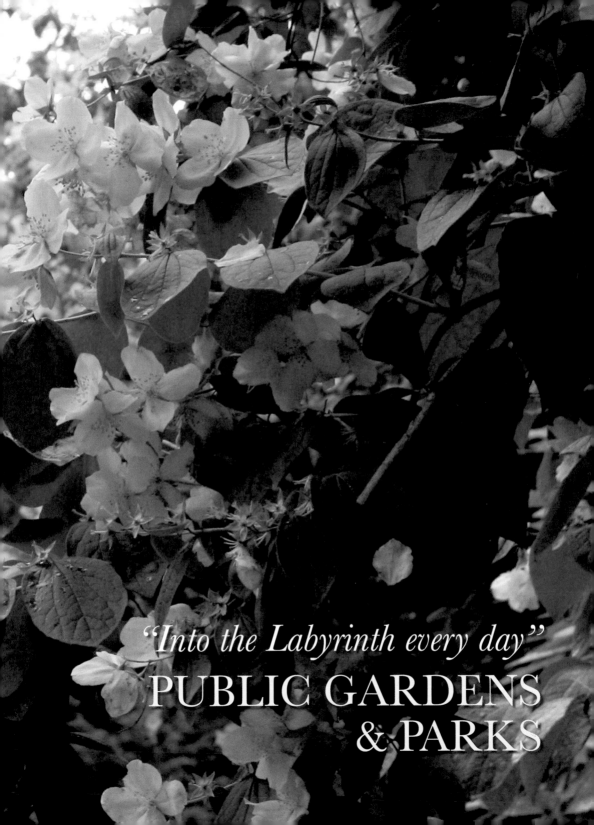

"Into the Labyrinth every day"
PUBLIC GARDENS
& PARKS

The Long Water at Kensington Gardens is now a bird sanctuary.

> *Fanny & I went into the Park yesterday & drove about*
> *& were very much entertained.*
> — Letter from Jane Austen to Cassandra, 7 March 1814

Jane Austen loved the outdoors. She relished driving in the country and enjoyed walking for hours, calling herself a "desperate walker." Jane Austen's heroines delight in being out-of-doors, too. They walk on the rolling green Devonshire downs in *Sense and Sensibility*, climb to Beechen Cliff in *Northanger Abbey*, and picnic at Box Hill in *Emma*. They make excursions to ruins and have an appreciation for the picturesque. Like Jane herself, they find some of their greatest happiness when they are in touch with nature.

Into the Park

Even away from the gardens and pleasure grounds of home, Jane Austen found ways to enjoy nature. In London, Kensington Gardens provided flower-filled, shady places to walk, and the lanes in Hyde Park were ideal for a drive. In Bath, Sydney Gardens had numerous paths and a labyrinth. Farther afield, Jane often drove or walked for pleasure to the small villages and viewpoints surrounding Bath:

I am just returned from my Airing in the very bewitching
Phaeton & four . . . . We . . . had a very pleasant drive:
One pleasure succeeds another rapidly.
— Letter from Jane Austen to Cassandra, 27 May 1801

The Great Parks of London

In Jane Austen's day, London's fashionable gardens and parks
were St. James Park, Green Park, Hyde Park, and Kensington
Gardens, all popular promenades or drives for the inhabitants of
the metropolis. St. James Park, though crowded with visitors, was
frequented less by the gentry, possibly because it was closer to the
merchant side of the city than the other parks, or perhaps because
of the "monotony and dulness of the old-fashioned avenues
without their magnificence, the trees being low, and of a stunted
growth," as American tourist Louis Simond reported. Green Park
was a little better, he said, but Hyde Park and Kensington Gardens,
connected to each other but separated by a ha-ha, were the most
desirable locations for the upper classes to see and be seen.

When Jane Austen wrote to Cassandra that "Fanny & I
went into the Park yesterday & drove about," she probably meant
Hyde Park, which was open to carriages and was popular both for
"taking the air" and for showing off socially. Both Hyde Park and
Kensington Gardens, where Jane liked to stroll, were within walking
distance of the houses her brother Henry owned at various times at Michael's Place, Sloane
Street, and Hans Place.

Sunday was a popular day for strolling about Kensington Gardens and meeting
acquaintances, as Jane Austen noted:

> The third day succeeding their knowledge of the particulars, was so fine, so
> beautiful a Sunday as to draw many to Kensington Gardens, though it was only
> the second week in March.
> — *Sense and Sensibility*

Jane Austen wrote the scene based on her own experiences—she liked walking in the greenery of
the gardens herself on fine Sundays:

> Your Lilacs are in leaf, *ours* are in bloom—The Horse chesnuts are quite out, &
> the Elms almost.—I had a pleasant walk in Kensington G[arden]s on Sunday with
> Henry, Mr Smith & Mr Tilson—everything was fresh & beautiful."
> — Letter from Jane Austen to Cassandra, 25 April 1811

The Long Water at Kensington Gardens viewed from the Italian Gardens

Hyde Park and Kensington Gardens

London
royalparks.org.uk

These two great historic parks of London cover a combined area of 760 acres. Features include magnificent formal avenues of trees, a lake, meadows, horse rides, and ornamental flower gardens. The parks are home to Speaker's Corner, the Italian Gardens, the Albert Memorial, a statue in honor of Peter Pan, the Serpentine Gallery, and the Diana, Princess of Wales Memorial Fountain. Visitors who find it difficult to see the entire area of the two parks on their own may schedule an hour-long tour drive around the parks in electric buggies with wheelchair facilities. Volunteers drive the buggies; the group is supported by donations. Bookings: Tel: +44 (0)7767 498 096. Further information: www.hydeparkappeal.org.

In the Garden with Jane Austen

Jane clearly relished the sight of the trees and flowering shrubs at Kensington Gardens. We know that at least one beautiful flowering shrub she loved grew there profusely—the syringa (mock orange).

> One of the great recommendations of this plant [syringa] is, that it will thrive in confined places, and under the shade and drip of trees, as may be particularly observed in the walks of Kensington gardens.
> — *Sylva Florifera*, 1823

Hyde Park

At the western extremity of Piccadilly, is open every day in the year from six in the morning till nine at night. No horseman is excluded; nor any carriage but hackney or stage coaches.

Kensington Gardens

Are connected with the western extremity of Hyde Park . . . . Viewed from Hyde Park, the rich foliage of these gardens are delightful, being separated only by a Ha-ha-wall. The promenade here and in Hyde Park in summer, presents a most interesting display of beauty and fashion. The gravel walks in this park are generally covered with horsemen and carriages; from two till five in the afternoon, with pedestrians, in great numbers, displaying a picture of content and enjoyment not exceeded in the environs of any court in Europe.

— *London: Being a Complete Guide to the British Capital*, 1814

Kensington Garden walking dresses for July 1807, from La Belle Assemblée

Sydney Gardens

The house the Austens chose when they moved to Bath, No. 4 Sydney Place, is directly opposite Sydney Gardens. The gardens, described in a guidebook of the time as being "laid out with uncommon taste," and having "plants and trees [that] flourish in beautiful luxuriance" soon became one of Jane's favorite walks:

> Yesterday was a busy day with me, or at least with my feet & my stockings; I was walking almost all day long; I went to Sydney Gardens soon after one, & did not return till four, & after dinner I walked to Weston.
> — Letter from Jane Austen to Cassandra, 21 April 1805

The leafy paths of the gardens provided Jane with a shady, cool retreat from the heats of summer in the city. She walked, too, along the canal that runs through the garden. A path borders the canal to this day, running under graceful iron footbridges with the date "1800" engraved on their arches.

Sydney Gardens, known as "The Vauxhall of Bath," after the great London pleasure garden, had numerous enticing attractions, including its famous labyrinth, a riding trail, swings, bowling-greens, and cold baths. Public breakfasts were held several times a week, at which the guests drank tea and ate, strolled around, chatted, and listened to music. Jane joked about these breakfasts in a letter to her sister while visiting in Bath.

There was a very long list of Arrivals here in the Newspaper yesterday, so that we need not immediately dread absolute Solitude; —& there is a public Breakfast in Sydney Gardens every morning, so that we shall not be wholly starved.
— Letter from Jane Austen to Cassandra, 17 May 1799

Grand galas were held several times each summer. These hugely popular entertainments included concerts and displays of fireworks and illuminations. Though Jane appreciated other forms of music, she wasn't thrilled by the gala concerts. The illuminations and fireworks, however, she loved:

There is to be a grand gala on tuesday evening in Sydney Gardens;—a Concert, with Illuminations & fireworks;—to the latter Eliz[abeth] & I look forward with pleasure, & even the Concert will have more than its' usual charm with me, as the Gardens are large enough for me to get pretty well beyond the reach of its sound.
— Letter from Jane Austen to Cassandra, 2 June 1799

Parties of Pleasure

Exploring parties, or "parties of pleasure," to beautiful outdoor sites and grand estates, were very popular in Jane Austen's day. Jane and her family often formed parties of pleasure to visit such sites of special interest and beauty as Beaulieu Abbey, Netley Abbey, the New Forest, and probably Box Hill, made so famous by the picnic there in *Emma*. Even trips to visit family members living several counties away afforded Jane with the opportunity to stop for a while and appreciate the surrounding countryside:

I was very much pleased with the Country in general—;—between Guildford & Ripley I thought it particularly pretty . . . the veiws were beautiful. I cannot say what we did *not* see, but I should think there could not be a Wood or a Meadow or a Palace or a remarkable spot in England that was not spread out before us, on one side or the other.
— Letter from Jane Austen to Cassandra, 20 May 1813

The characters in Jane Austen's novels enjoy touring about as well. In *Sense and Sensibility*, Sir John Middleton, who counts a day without a party as lost, constantly arranges little excursions: "He was a blessing to all the juvenile part of the neighbourhood, for in summer he was for ever

The canal at Sydney Gardens, Bath. "Last night we walked by the Canal." — Jane Austen, May 6, 1801

Sydney Gardens

Pulteney Street, Bath
cityofbath.co.uk, under
    "Parks & Rec"

Sydney Gardens, the oldest park in the city of Bath, was
laid out in 1795. The labyrinth was removed long ago,
but the essential layout of the park remains the same
as when Jane Austen walked there. One of the many
winding paths follows the canal through the park.

Victoria Park, Bath

In the Garden with Jane Austen

Royal Victoria Park

Bath
bathnes.gov.uk, under "Environment and Planning"

The Royal Victoria Park is at the bottom of the hill below The Royal Crescent, on the site of the field where Jane Austen walked when conditions in the Crescent weren't pleasant. "We did not walk long in the Crescent yesterday," she wrote to Cassandra in 1805, "It was hot and not crowded enough; so we went into the field."

The park, open since 1830 and occupying nearly 60 acres, boasts large botanical gardens containing an outstanding collection of trees, shrubs, and flowers. In addition to walks and drives, its numerous recreational facilities include a skateboard park and a children's play area, bowling greens, putting and golf greens, tennis courts, an aviary, and a model boating pond.

Alexandra Park at Beechen Cliff

Bath
cityofbath.co.uk, under "Parks & Rec"

Alexandra Park is situated at the top of Beechen Cliff, which Jane Austen called "that noble hill whose beautiful verdure and hanging coppice render it so striking an object from almost every opening in Bath." The top of the cliff provides breathtaking views of Bath. In *Northanger Abbey*, the heroine, Catherine Morland, walks to Beechen Cliff with her beloved Henry Tilney and his sister, Eleanor. The path to the top of the cliff is scenic, but Catherine is absorbed with Henry. He gives her a fine lecture on the picturesque, that is, whether a view would make a good painting. "They talked of foregrounds, distances, second distances, side-screens and perspective, lights and shades, and Catherine was so hopeful a scholar, that when they gained the top of Beechen Cliff, she voluntarily rejected the whole city of Bath as unworthy to make part of a landscape."

Access to the park is up the long flight of steps known as Jacob's Ladder, or by car from Shakespeare Avenue.

forming parties to eat cold ham and chicken out of doors . . . ." He wants to arrange something of the same kind for the Dashwood sisters:

> A party was formed this evening for going on the following day to see a very fine place about twelve miles from Barton. . . . The grounds were declared to be highly beautiful . . . . They contained a noble piece of water; a sail on which was to a form a great part of the morning's amusement; cold provisions were to be taken, open carriages only to be employed, and every thing conducted in the usual style of a complete party of pleasure.

The Box Hill Picnic

Box Hill is set in the beautiful, rolling countryside of Surrey, near where Jane Austen imagined *Emma* as taking place. In Jane's time, the hill, only 25 miles outside London, was a popular goal for city-dwellers looking to commune a little with nature. The views from the top of Box Hill are spectacular, making it the perfect spot for a picnic. Jane never recorded whether she actually visited Box Hill herself, but she is famous for writing only what she knew. When the Austen family traveled to and from Jane's brother Edward's estate in Godmersham, Kent, they sometimes stayed with cousins who lived a mere five miles from the famous hill, at Great Bookham, Surrey. It seems reasonable to believe that the Cooke family may have taken the Austen family on a special party of pleasure to Box Hill.

In *Emma*, the ladies and gentlemen of Highbury plan a picnic excursion to Box Hill. The heroine, Emma Woodhouse, wishes for the Box Hill outing "to be done in a quiet, unpretending, elegant way," but after the pretentious Mrs. Elton gets involved, it is inevitable that the elegance degenerates into "the bustle and preparation, the regular eating and drinking, and picnic parade of the Eltons . . . ." The outing starts out well but soon sours.

Garden Recipes for Parties of Pleasure

In Jane Austen's time, fashionable society considered a tan unattractive, as they associated it with outdoor labor. (In *Pride and Prejudice*, Bingley's snobbish sisters mock Elizabeth Bennet for the tan she acquires while touring.) Ladies hoping to avoid a tan might have used these recipes.

A Preservative from Tanning.
INFUSE in clean Water for three days a pound of Lupines, then take them out, and boil them in a copper vessel with five quarts of fresh Water. When the Lupines are boiled tender, and the Water grows rather ropy, press out the Liquor, and keep it for use. Whenever you are under a necessity of exposing yourself to the sun, wash the face and neck with this preparation.

An excellent Receipt to clear a tanned Complexion.
AT night going to rest, bathe the face with the Juice of Strawberries, and let it lie on the part all night, and in the morning wash yourself with Chervil Water. The skin will soon become fair and smooth.
— *The Toilet of Flora*, 1799

View from Box Hill

Box Hill

The Old Fort, Box Hill Road,
Box Hill, Tadworth, Surrey
Tel. +44 (0)1306 885502
nationaltrust.org.uk

Box Hill, the site of the famous picnic in *Emma*, features
outstanding views of the surrounding woodland and downs
of Surrey. Features include nature trails where a dozen
varieties of wild orchids grow, picnic areas, and a visitors'
center with a café.

They had a very fine day for Box Hill; and all the other outward circumstances . . . were in favour of a pleasant party. . . . Nothing was wanting but to be happy when they got there. . . . Seven miles were travelled in expectation of enjoyment, and every body had a burst of admiration on first arriving; but . . . there was deficiency. There was a languor, a want of spirits, a want of union, which could not be got over. . . . Even Emma grew tired at last . . . and wished herself rather walking quietly about with any of the others, or sitting almost alone, and quite unattended to, in tranquil observation of the beautiful views beneath her.

Tours of the Picturesque

In Jane Austen's time, the fashion for the romantic, the gothic, and the picturesque reached fever-pitch levels. With it came an increased appreciation for the artistic beauty of antiquities and ruins. Stumps of castles, blown apart in the English Civil War, and shells of abbeys, abandoned since Henry VIII's day, had previously been seen only as sources of free building materials. Now they had a new appeal: the picturesque object.

William Gilpin, a clergyman and author whom Jane Austen was said to admire, set the tone with his essays on the picturesque, defining it as "that kind of beauty which is agreeable in a picture." Rough, twisted, broken scenes were to be preferred to regular, smooth beauty. Ruins answered the purpose delightfully. Ladies and gentlemen, sketchbooks and journals in hand, made special trips to view hoary old ruins. In *Pride and Prejudice*, Elizabeth Bennet and her aunt and uncle the Gardiners visit several tourist sites before they arrive at Mr. Darcy's estate, Pemberley, in Derbyshire. Guidebooks of the day suggested many worthy attractions in the areas they visited. In Oxford they might have toured the Botanic Garden, in Birmingham the

Dr. Syntax takes a tumble while sketching a castle ruin.

A tour of the picturesque

William Gilpin and his principles of the picturesque were humorously satirized in a series of books that we know Jane Austen read and enjoyed, *The Three Tours of Dr. Syntax*. In the series, Dr. Syntax, a poor parson, sets out to make his fortune describing the picturesque:

"I'll make a TOUR—and then I'll WRITE IT.
You well know what my pen can do,
And I'll employ my pencil too:—
I'll ride and write, and sketch and print,
And thus create a real mint;
I'll prose it here, I'll verse it there,
And picturesque it everywhere."
— *The Tour of Dr. Syntax in Search of the Picturesque*, 1812

Netley Abbey

innovative new factories. Warwick Castle, an imposing structure set in grounds designed by Humphry Repton, and Blenheim, a huge baroque palace, were popular tourist destinations. Kenilworth was "a vast and magnificent pile of ruins," according to one 1815 guidebook, well worth a visit for lovers of the picturesque.

Netley Abbey

Southampton, where the Austen women lived after leaving Bath, was surrounded by fine country containing many attractions worth exploring. Among the popular sites that drew tourists were the naval dockyards, the New Forest, Beaulieu Abbey, and Netley Abbey. Netley was particularly famous. Originally a monastery founded in 1239, the abbey, partly ruined and extremely picturesque, was irresistible to sentimental tourists. Its cloisters were filled with trees and ivy clung to its walls, enhancing the noble, decayed look. Innumerable drawings and engravings were made of the abbey, and many a poem indulged in "mournful plainings over the fallen splendor." There was even an operatic farce about it, performed in Covent Garden in 1794.

The abbey was a favorite destination for the Austens, a treat to be shared when their extended family came to visit. Jane Austen's niece made note of a trip to Netley while visiting Southampton:

We all except G'mama took a boat & went to Netley Abby the ruins of which look beautiful. We eat there of some biscuits we had taken, & returned quite delighted. Aunt Jane & I walked in the High Street till late.
— Diary of Fanny Knight, 16 September, 1807

To Miss Austen, the following Ode to Pity is dedicated, from a thorough knowledge of her pitiful Nature, by her obedt humle Servt The Author

Ode to Pity
1.
Ever musing I delight to tread
The Paths of honour and the Myrtle Grove
Whilst the pale Moon her beams doth shed
On disappointed Love.
While Philomel on airy hawthorn Bush
Sings sweet and Melancholy, And the thrush
Converses with the Dove.
2.
Gently brawling down the turnpike road,
Sweetly noisy falls the Silent Stream—
The Moon emerges from behind a Cloud
And darts upon the Myrtle Grove her beam.
Ah! then what Lovely Scenes appear,
The hut, the Cot, the Grot, and Chapel queer,
And eke the Abbey too a mouldering heap,
Conceal'd by aged pines her head doth rear
And quite invisible doth take a peep.
— Written by Jane Austen as a teenager

Netley Abbey ruins

Netley Abbey Ruins

Netley Abbey, Hampshire
netleyabbey.info
english-heritage.org.uk

Today, English Heritage maintains the Netley Abbey ruins as an ancient monument. The trees and ivy have been cleared away, and some of the more vulnerable walls have been stabilized. Tours of the ruins are self-guided. Free, downloadable MP3 audio clips for touring the abbey are available at the english-heritage. org Netley Abbey website.

A rustic seat a Gilbert White's House

"I could not do without a Syringa"

RE-CREATING JANE
AUSTEN'S GARDEN

"Rustic seats innumerable" are appropriate for the cottage garden.

Some of the Flower seeds are coming up very well—but your Mignionette makes a wretched appearance.—Miss Benn has been equally unlucky as to hers; She has seed from 4 different people, & none of it comes up.
— Letter from Jane Austen to Cassandra, 29 May 1811

The quaint cottage garden, the elegant villa garden, and the breathtaking grounds and gardens of the great estates all appear in Jane Austen's novels. How to begin re-creating them? What plants were grown by the gardeners of the day and where did they grow them? What would the flower gardens have looked like, and where exactly should one place a shrubbery? It is possible to create your very own "Jane Austen garden." Grow hyacinths for Catherine Morland of *Northanger Abbey* and geraniums for Fanny Price of *Mansfield Park.* Design paths and winding ways that Marianne Dashwood of *Sense and Sensibility* would delight in losing herself in. Plant a shrubbery that would make Emma and Mr. Knightley happy and grow a rose garden for Lady Bertram and Pug. Sow mignonette seed for Cassandra Austen and raise

gooseberries for Mrs. Austen. Most important, plant Jane Austen's favorite syringa "for the sake of Cowper's line" and for her.

Fortunately, it is now quite simple to stock your own garden in imitation of those of the eighteenth century: true cottage gardens, gardens similar to Jane Austen's at Steventon and Chawton, and even the gardens of such great estates as Pemberley. Local nurseries and garden centers sometimes carry heirloom varieties, but if not, the Internet provides easy access to places that do. Searches for terms such as "heritage" or "heirloom" seeds, flowers, and plants turn up numerous nurseries and mail-order catalogues. There are also groups specializing in saving and trading heirloom seeds that generally welcome new members.

The look of a garden of Jane Austen's time also can be achieved with modern varieties. Almost everything grown in her day is available now, if not an eighteenth-century cultivar, then one close in appearance. Modern cultivars are also often disease resistant.

Re-creating the Cottage Garden

The hallmark of a cottage garden is its casual, mixed style. True cottage gardens in Jane Austen's time mingled fruit, vegetables, vines, trees, and flowers—utility and beauty together. Beauty being subjective, however, modern cottage gardeners may want to pick and choose what "authentic" components of the eighteenth-century cottage garden they add to their own gardens. Neatly trained fruit trees, twining honeysuckle, roses, herbs intermixed with flowers, even attractive vegetables all add to the atmosphere of a charming modern cottage garden. Pigsties, dung heaps, and outhouses can probably be dispensed with.

The cottage gardens in Georgian and Regency times were surrounded by wooden fences (usually whitewashed or painted in shades of green, ochre red, or brown), hedges, or stone or brick walls, all of which served to keep the chickens in, and fences in any of these forms would be appropriate to the modern cottage garden. Fruit trees may be grown in their natural form if there is room, but the classic eighteenth-century method, especially in confined quarters, was to espalier the trees, that is, train them flat to the garden walls or sometimes to the cottage or house walls, generally in a fan shape. The espalier method allows the trees to gain reflected warmth from the walls and leads to a larger crop, always a goal for the practical cottager. It is possible today to purchase trees from nurseries that have already begun the espalier training process. Certain fruit bushes may be grown as attractive standards, particularly gooseberries and currants. Standards (with one thick stem that makes the plant resemble a small tree) not only have a more decorative shape, but it also is easier to weed under them. We know the

The rose garden at Chawton Cottage

Austen women grew gooseberry "trees" in their gardens, as Mrs. Austen mentions them in a letter to her granddaughter.

Vegetables in a modern cottage garden can be mixed right in the garden with the flowers. Many forms of vegetables are quite decorative and make attractive, authentic additions to the modern cottage garden. Indeed, several types of food-producing plants started their British garden lives in the flower garden. Gardening books of Jane Austen's time list eggplant or aubergine and peppers in the flower garden, and tomatoes (called also "love apples") in both the flower and kitchen gardens. In addition to "merely" ornamental flowers, some flowers can be grown that have the same practical uses they had in Jane Austen's day. Marigolds, for example, make pleasant borders to vegetable beds and act as natural insect deterrents. The kitchen garden at Chawton House uses marigolds in this way.

To upgrade the true cottager's garden to a genteel cottage garden such as the Dashwoods had at Barton Cottage in *Sense and Sensibility*, it is only necessary to replace the cabbages in front with a little green turfed area, plant only decorative trees there, and banish the chickens and anything else utilitarian to the back of the house.

Plan of a rose garden from An Encyclopaedia of Gardening, *1822.*

Some of the Roses Grown at Chawton Cottage

Rosa "Blush Noisette"
Rosa alba "Belle Amour"
Rosa centifolia
  "Shailers White Moss"
Rosa gallica "Gloire de France"
Rosa gallica officinalis
  "Portland Rose"
Rosa gallica versicolor
  (Rosa Mundi)

The Chawton Cottage kitchen garden

The Chawton Cottage Kitchen Garden

The kitchen garden at Chawton Cottage features heritage varieties of vegetables, fruit, and herbs. The beans and peas are grown up natural, wooden sticks and string, and only organic methods are used. Seashells strung on string provide an attractive "scarecrow" for the garden. The varieties grown in the Cottage kitchen garden are:

Seashells scare away the birds in the kitchen garden at Chawton Cottage.

Potatoes (Solanum tuberosum)
Cucumbers (Cucumis sativa)
Runner beans (Phaseolus coccineus "Painted Lady")
Melons
Marrows (Squash)
Pumpkins
Carrots (Daucus carota)

Rhubarb (Rheum rhaponticum)
Parsnips "White Gem"
Beetroots "Bolthardy"
Radishes "French Breakfast"
Coriander (Coriandrum sativum)
Peas (Pisum sativum)
Onions (Allium cepa)
Garlic (Allium sativum)
Tomatoes (Lycospersicum esculentum)

A 6 by 6 foot section of a flower border at Chawton Cottage

A Chawton Cottage Flower Border

The original form of Jane Austen's garden at Chawton Cottage is mostly unknown. Part of the property was sold over the years, and a large hedge planted roughly 50 years ago further obscures the original outlines of the garden. The current garden is a lovely interpretation that includes the flowers, vines, and vegetables the Austen family could have grown or would have seen in the gardens of their relatives and friends. The garden includes a shrubbery, a rose garden, a kitchen garden, a dye garden, and flower borders. Virtually all the varieties grown today at the Cottage were available during Jane Austen's time or earlier. The head gardener at Chawton Cottage, Celia Simpson, has kindly provided a sample 6 by 6 foot (1.8 by 1.8 meters) flower border as grown at the Cottage:

Alcea filicifolia (Hollyhock)
Alchemilla mollis (Lady's Mantle)
Allium christophii (Star of Persia)
Alyssum saxatile (Basket of Gold, Gold Alyssum)
Astrantia major (Masterwort)
Dianthus barbatus (Sweet William)
Dianthus superbus (Superb Pink, Large Pink)
Dicentra spectabilis (Bleeding Heart)

Geranium "Buxton Blue" (Garden Geranium, Hardy Geranium, Cranesbill – "Buxton Blue")
Helenium autumnale "The Bishop" (Sneezeweed, Helen's Flower, Dogtooth Daisy – "The Bishop")
Hemerocallis "Little Maid" (Daylily "Little Maid")
Lilium candidum (Madonna Lily)
Lonicera fragrantissima (Winter Honeysuckle)
Lonicera halliana (Hall's Honeysuckle)
Lunaria annua (Money Plant, Honesty, Moonwort, Silver Dollar)
Lychnis chalcedonica (Maltese Cross, Nonesuch)
Hemerocallis flava (Yellow Daylily, Lemon Lily, Custard Lily)
Oenothera biennis (Evening Primrose)
Phlox paniculata (Garden Phlox)
Polemonium caeruleum (Jacob's Ladder)
Rosa alba "Belle Amour" (Alba Rose "Belle Amour")
Rosa centifolia "Shailers White Moss" (Moss Rose "Shailers White Moss")
Rudbeckia sullivantii "Goldsturm" (Black-eyed Susan "Goldsturm")
Sisyrinchium striata (Satin Flower, Yellow-eyed Grass)
Thalictrum aquilegifolium (Columbine Meadow Rue)
Veronicastrum virginicum alba (Culver's Root, white)

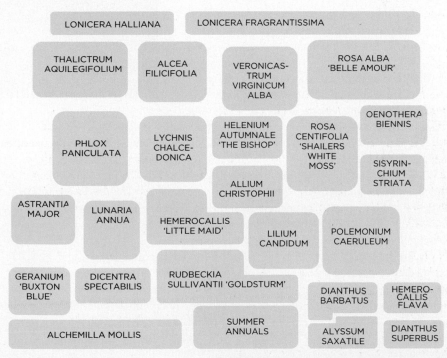

The planting plan for one section of the Chawton Cottage garden

Re-creating the Villa or Small Mansion House Garden

Many modern suburban properties are perfect places for experimenting with eighteenth- and early-nineteenth-century garden design ideas. Often newly carved from former farm fields, they are nearly blank canvases, ready for the owners to "project shrubberies, and invent a sweep," as do Elinor and Edward, the heroine and hero of *Sense and Sensibility*. What better way to fill those acres of endless lawn than with a shrubbery?

Pot Marigolds

Villas had most of the garden features of the great estates, just on a smaller scale: shrubberies, flower gardens, conservatories, even decorative outbuildings in the form of temples or rustic structures. Any of these would be appropriate to a modern property, if adapted properly.

Shrubberies can be planted as they often were at villas, around the sides of the property to provide a screen from any neighboring house that might happen to be too close. To plant a shrubbery properly, plant it in a tiered fashion rising from the path, just like a flower border—shorter plants and flowers in the front, then flowering shrubs, then the trees in back. A shrubbery may be closed, that is, planted fairly thickly on both sides as a wooded walk, though if that is done it is important (by eighteenth-century standards) to allow for occasional vistas and viewpoints. Or plant an open shrubbery, on one side of the path only, with the inner side (toward the central lawn)

Peony

mostly open, but plant some spaced trees on that side to provide shade for the walkers without obstructing the view.

Paths through the shrubbery can be made of gravel or sand, as they were in Jane Austen's day, or some modern possibilities might be paths of pine needles or shredded bark. They should be serpentine, follow a circular route (cul-de-sacs were considered in poor taste), and lead to tastefully chosen viewpoints, or to decorative structures. Garden seats scattered along the paths are in perfect character, as are little flower beds carved out of the lawn and filled to look like flower baskets. A flower bed can be tucked as a surprise in the center of a grove of trees planted around a section of a path. Gardeners in an earlier-eighteenth-century mood can place urns, obelisks, busts, and statues at carefully chosen points along the paths, with seats for contemplation of the Latin inscriptions or sentimental poetry inscribed on the decorative objects.

The walled kitchen garden at Houghton Lodge now houses attractive flower gardens.

The Gardens of Houghton Lodge

The owner of Houghton Lodge reports that when the restoration of the gardens at Houghton Lodge was begun, the garden designer often chose modern varieties of the flowers grown in Jane Austen's time, close in appearance and color, but stronger and more disease resistant. She has kindly provided the following sample of flowers grown in the attractive borders at Houghton Lodge:

Delphiniums
Honeysuckle
Irises
Lupins
Mignonette
Peonies
Philadelphus (Mock Orange)
Pinks
Roses
Violets

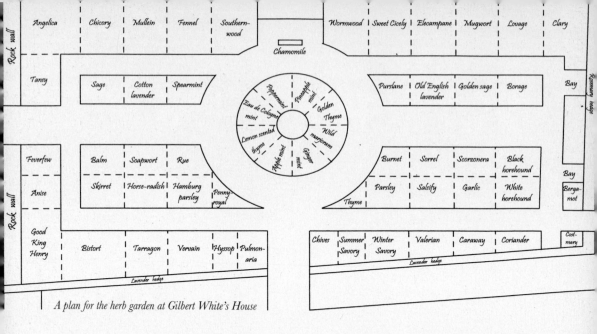

A plan for the herb garden at Gilbert White's House

The Herb Garden at Gilbert White's House

The herb garden at Gilbert White's House is a lovely example of the geometric style of planting. Herbs grow in neat rows surrounding another, circular bed of herbs with a tall, decorative jar at the center. A garden seat is conveniently placed for enjoying the sight and fragrances of the many traditional herbs, which include both culinary and medicinal varieties. The head gardener, David Standing, has kindly provided a list of the herbs growing in the garden:

Angelica	Costmary	Lovage	Sorrel
Anise	Cotton Lavender	Mugwort	Southernwood
Apple Mint	Eau de Cologne Mint	Mullein	Spearmint
Balm	Elecampane	Parsley	Summer Savory
Bay	English Lavender	Pennyroyal	Sweet Cicely
Bergamot	Fennel	Peppermint	Tansy
Bistort	Feverfew	Pineapple Mint	Tarragon
Black Horehound	Garlic	Pulmonaria	Thyme
Borage	Ginger Mint	Purslane	Valerian
Burnet	Golden Sage	Rosemary	Vervain
Caraway	Golden Thyme	Rue	White Horehound
Chamomile	Good King Henry	Sage	Wild Marjoram
Chicory	Hamburg Parsley	Salsify	Winter Savory
Chives	Horse-radish	Scorzonera	Wormwood
Clary	Hyssop	Skirret	
Coriander	Lemon Scented Thyme	Soapwort	

The herb garden at Gilbert White's House

Re-creating the Great Estate Garden

If you're fortunate enough to have your own Pemberley, you may want to hire your own modern Humphry Repton. Professional landscape designers have the expertise to execute your vision on a large scale, making "everything as complete as possible . . . shrubberies and flower-gardens, and rustic seats innumerable"—and worthy of a Mr. Darcy. The beauty of having a large piece of property to work with is that it is possible to have most of the trappings of a large eighteenth- or early-nineteenth-century estate: conservatories and fountains, extensive pleasure grounds with serpentine paths leading through leafy, flowering shrubberies, flower beds set in smooth green lawns, streams "of some natural importance . . . swelled into greater," even a ha-ha with some sheep on the other side if ordinances permit.

A colorful flower border lines the walled kitchen garden at Stoneleigh Abbey.

The Gardens of Stoneleigh Abbey

The beautiful flower borders at Stoneleigh Abbey contain some newer cultivars and are thus a modern interpretation of the borders that would have been grown during Jane Austen's time. A sample of the flowers grown in a border at Stoneleigh Abbey was kindly provided by the gardener:

The medieval gatehouse and flower borders at Stoneleigh Abbey

Hesperis matronalis (Sweet Rocket) 30" high and 24" expansion
Digitalis purpurea (Foxglove) 72" high and 24" expansion
Achillea ptarmica "The Pearl" (Sneezewort) 30" high and 30" diameter
Hyssopus officinalis (Hyssop) 24" high and 36" expansion
Stachys officinalis (Wood Betony) 24" high and 18" expansion
Lavandula Angustifolia (English Lavender) 24" high and 30" expansion

Re-creating the Town or City Garden

Modern practice seems to be changing in town gardens, with possessors of even the smallest open space tucked behind a townhouse adopting an informal, asymmetrical style. This would have seemed odd to people in Jane Austen's day. In their opinion, the only thing to be done with a small space, especially a flat one where the whole of it could be seen at a glance, was to render it as neat and tidy as possible. Symmetry was allowed, even encouraged, in small spaces, as being more in character with spaces usually surrounded by walls; a modern town gardener looking to re-create a Georgian or Regency Garden will want to plant according to a geometric plan. A common design for the garden behind the house was to place flower borders under the walls, then lay a flagstone or gravel path neatly circling an interior patch of turf or gravel, which sometimes had flower beds cut into it. Two excellent examples of this style may be seen in Bath, at the Georgian Garden, No. 4 The Circus (discussed in Chapter 3), and the Kennard Garden at The Kennard, a hotel. Both sites are excellent sources of inspiration for re-creating an authentic Georgian town garden.

Clematis

Daylily

Some townhouses then had no green garden in back at all, their owners choosing instead to pave the area for ease of carrying out household chores. There are older houses in the centers of towns today that still have only paved areas, and unless the pavement is dug up, no traditional garden is possible. In that case, or in apartments and flats, the proper look can be achieved with potted flowers and window boxes, which have their own charm. Stenciling Georgian or Regency geometric designs on the pots will give them that Jane Austen-era feeling.

If there is a bit of space in front on the street side, an equally formal look is appropriate. Garden plans for the fronts of town houses of the time usually show just a few design options: a straight path to the front door, on the far left, far right, or down the center. The remainder of the area should be planted with grass, with optional straight flower borders as edging or small, neat flower beds cut into the turf.

We make our gardens today for the same reasons and with the same enjoyment that Jane Austen did. Whichever style you choose for your garden, let it be for you, as it was for Jane Austen, a place of refreshment and renewal.

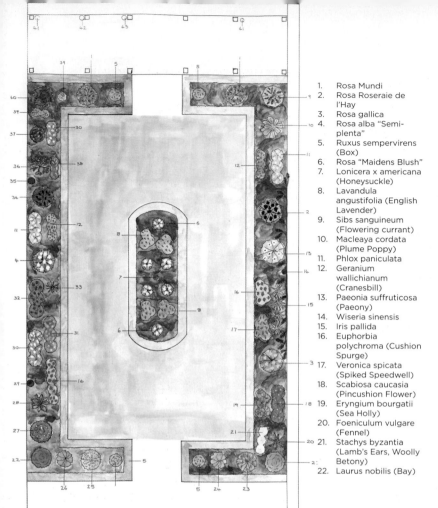

1. Rosa Mundi
2. Rosa Roseraie de l'Hay
3. Rosa gallica
4. Rosa alba "Semi-plenta"
5. Ruxus sempervirens (Box)
6. Rosa "Maidens Blush"
7. Lonicera x americana (Honeysuckle)
8. Lavandula angustifolia (English Lavender)
9. Sibs sanguineum (Flowering currant)
10. Macleaya cordata (Plume Poppy)
11. Phlox paniculata
12. Geranium wallichianum (Cranesbill)
13. Paeonia suffruticosa (Paeony)
14. Wiseria sinensis
15. Iris pallida
16. Euphorbia polychroma (Cushion Spurge)
17. Veronica spicata (Spiked Speedwell)
18. Scabiosa caucasia (Pincushion Flower)
19. Eryngium bourgatii (Sea Holly)
20. Foeniculum vulgare (Fennel)
21. Stachys byzantia (Lamb's Ears, Woolly Betony)
22. Laurus nobilis (Bay)
23. Rosmarinus officinalis (Rosemary)
24. Salvia officinalis (Common Sage)
25. Santolina chamaecyparris (Cotton Lavender)
26. Salvia officinalis "Purpurescens" (Purple Sage)
27. Daphne odora
28. Mahonia aquifolium
29. Malus "Egremont Russet" (Apple)
30. Zantedechia aethiopica (Arum or Calla lily)
31. Astrantia major (Masterwort)
32. Geranium pratense (Meadow Cranesbill)
33. Dicentra bacchanal
34. Fuchia magellanica (Lady's Eardrops)
35. Pyrus (Pear)
36. Forsythia
37. Viburnum tinus
38. Digitalis purpurea (Foxglove)
39. Digitalis lanata
40. Ilex aquifolium (Common Holly)
41. Vitus vinifera (Grape Vine)
42. Clematic orientale
43. Jasminium officinale (Jasmine)

The planting plan for the Kennard Hotel garden

The Kennard Hotel Garden

The owners of the Kennard Hotel have created a charming, authentic interpretation of a Georgian town garden, using heirloom varieties of flowers, trees, herbs, and vines. They have kindly provided a list of the plants and trees grown in their garden:

Astrantia major (Masterwort)
Buxus sempervirens (Box)
Clematis orientale (Oriental Clematis)
Daphne odora (Winter Daphne)
Dicentra bacchanal (Bleeding Heart)

Digitalis lanata (Grecian Foxglove)
Digitalis purpurea (Foxglove)
Eryngium bourgatii (Sea Holly)
Euphorbia polychrome (Cushion Spurge)
Foeniculum vulgare (Fennel)

Forsythia
Fuchsia magellanica (Lady's Eardrops, Hardy Fuchsia)
Geranium pretense (Meadow Cranesbill)
Geranium wallichianum (Cranesbill)
Ilex aquifolium (Common Holly)
Iris pallida (Sweet Iris)
Jasminium officinale (Jasmine)
Laurus nobilis (Sweet Bay)
Lavandula angustifolia (English Lavender)
Lonicera x Americana (Honeysuckle)
Macleaya cordata (Plume Poppy)
Mahonia aquifolium (Oregon Grape, Holly-Leaved Barberry)
Malus "Egremont Russet" (Apple)
Paeonia suffruticosa (Peony)
Phlox paniculata (Garden Phlox)
Pyrus (Pear)

Ribes sanguineum (Flowering Currant)
Rosa "Maidens Blush"
Rosa alba "Semi-plena"
Rosa "Gallica"
Rosa "Mundi"
Rosa "Roseraie de l'Hay"
Rosmarinus officinalis (Rosemary)
Salvia officinalis "Purpurescens" (Purple Sage)
Salvia officinalis (Common Sage)
Santolina chamaecyparris (Cotton Lavender)
Scabiosa caucasia (Pincushion Flower)
Stachys byzantia (Lamb's Ears, Woolly Betony)
Veronica spicata (Spiked Speedwell)
Viburnum tinus (Laurustinus)
Vitus vinifera (Grape Vine)
Wisteria sinensis (Chinese wisteria)
Zantedechia aethiopica (Arum or Calla Lily)

The Kennard Hotel

No. 11 Henrietta Street, Bath
Tel: +44 (0)1225 310472
kennard.co.uk

The Kennard Hotel garden

When the current owners of the Kennard Hotel purchased it in 2006, they were stymied by an apparent waste area in the back of the house, filled with a shed and overgrown vegetation that reached nearly to the top of the building. They set out to re-create a Georgian garden there, faithful to the 1794 period of the house. Their main inspiration, they say, has been the writing of Jane Austen. Her inspiration, combined with meticulous historical research, has enabled them to create a space where one can imagine her characters or even Jane herself strolling. The garden features flower borders under the garden walls, a graveled walking area in the center with a flower bed and a honeysuckle pole in the center, and gothic arches at the end of the garden leading to a quiet seating area, complete with a flower-filled urn. The plants and flowers are all appropriate to the era.

The Kennard Hotel garden is open to hotel guests and by special arrangement.

Gardens Featured in Jane Austen Film Adaptations

Pemberley, Longbourn, Hartfield, Mansfield Park—who wouldn't want to visit them in person, walk where Lizzy Bennet and Darcy walked, stroll through the shrubbery with Emma and Mr. Knightley, or sit gazing over the ha-ha with Fanny Price? The film adaptations of Jane Austen's novels bring them to life, allowing us a treasured glimpse of her world. Many of the sites used for filming are open for tours, and some of them have exquisite gardens that are well worth a visit.

SENSE AND SENSIBILITY
2008, starring Hattie Morahan, Charity Wakefield, and Dan Stevens

Blackpool Mill Cottage (Barton Cottage), Hartland Abbey, Hartland, Bideford, North Devon, Tel: +44 (0)1237 441264/234, hartlandabbey.com
> This 15th-century cottage, on the grounds of Hartland Abbey, is in a sheltered valley overlooking a cove. A holiday cottage, it is available to rent. The gardens of 12th-century abbey itself are open for tour. Gardens include four 18th-century walled gardens and restored Gertrude Jekyll gardens: the Baronet's Bog Garden, the Victorian Fernery, and the Camellia Garden.

Ham House (Cleveland), Richmond, Surrey, Tel: +44 (0)20 8940 1950, nationaltrust.org.uk
> A grand 17th-century house set alongside the river Thames, Ham House is supposed to be one of the most haunted houses in Britain. The formal gardens, which include famous lavender parterres, are unique examples of 17th-century garden design and are currently being restored.

Loseley Park (Barton Park), Guildford, Surrey, Tel: +44 (0)1483 304440, loseley-park.com
> Loseley House, originally built in the 1560s for a visit from Elizabeth I, features many gardens, including the award-winning Rose Garden with over one thousand old-fashioned rose bushes, the White Garden, an herb garden, a flower garden, an organic vegetable garden emphasizing heritage varieties, and a wildflower meadow.

SENSE AND SENSIBILITY
1995, starring Emma Thompson, Kate Winslet, and Hugh Grant

Compton Castle (Combe Magna), Marldon, Paignton, Devon, Tel: +44 (0)1803 843235, nationaltrust.org.uk
> Compton is a 600-year-old castle, complete with towers, curtain walls, and a portcullis. Hidden behind the fortified walls are delightful flower gardens and an herb garden in the inner courtyard.

Montacute House (Cleveland), Montacute, Somerset, Tel: +44 (0)1935 823289, nationaltrust.org.uk
> Montacute House is a grand Elizabethan stone house set in a 300-acre estate, most of which is

open to the public. Special garden features include ancient yew hedges, colorful flower borders, and two "pudding houses," where the hosts and their guests would retire to eat dessert in the garden.

Saltram House, (Norland Park), Plympton, Plymouth, Devon,

Tel: +44 (0)1752 333500, nationaltrust.org.uk

An imposing Georgian mansion featuring Robert Adam interiors, Saltram House is set in a magnificently landscaped park featuring follies and beautiful gardens. Frances, the third countess, corresponded with Jane Austen.

Wilton House, (ball scene), Wilton, Salisbury, Wiltshire,

Tel: +44 (0)1722 746714, wiltonhouse.co.uk

Wilton House, a 12th-century former abbey, is set in 21 acres of parkland and gardens, including a rose garden, a water garden, woodland walks, and a riverside walk leading to a Palladian bridge.

PRIDE AND PREJUDICE

2005, starring Keira Knightley and Matthew Macfadyen

Basildon Park (Netherfield Park), Lower Basildon, Reading, Berkshire, Tel: +44 (0)118 984 3040 nationaltrust.org.uk

Basildon Park is a magnificent 18th-century house set on the banks of the River Thames. The grounds of the Palladian mansion feature marked trails that wind through the beautiful parkland. The early 19th-century pleasure grounds are now being restored.

Burghley House (Rosings Park), Stamford, Lincolnshire, Tel: +44 (0)1780 752451, burghley.co.uk

Burghley, an impressive stone 16th-century house, is set in a landscape park designed by Capability Brown in the 18th century. The gardens include a sculpture garden, a rose garden, and the new Historical Garden of Surprises, containing water features, mazes, a moss house, and a grotto.

Chatsworth House (Pemberley), See the listing in Chapter 2.

Groombridge Place (Longbourn), Groombridge, Kent, Tel: +44 (0)1892 861444 , groombridge.co.uk

Groombridge Place, a pleasant 17th-century house constructed of warm red brick, is surrounded by gardens that range from 17th century formal gardens through 20th-century additions. Among the many gardens are a knot garden, a secret garden, a white rose garden, a herbaceous border, and an oriental garden. A special attraction is the "Enchanted Forest."

Stourhead (Darcy's first proposal - at the Temple of Apollo), Stourton, Warminster, Wiltshire

Tel: +44 (0)1747 841152, nationaltrust.org.uk

Stourhead, a majestic Palladian mansion, is set in a breathtaking 18th-century landscape garden that is justly world-famous. One of the first estates to break away from the rigid formality of earlier gardens, the grounds are full of walks that lead to exquisite temples and monuments, including the Temple of Flora, the Temple of Apollo, a Palladian bridge, and gothic ruins.

Wilton House, (Pemberley's drawing room), See the entry under *Sense and Sensibility*, 1995.

PRIDE AND PREJUDICE
1995, starring Jennifer Ehle and Colin Firth

Belton House (Rosings), Grantham, Lincolnshire, Tel: +44 (0)1476 566116, nationaltrust.org.uk
Belton house, an excellent model of Restoration architecture, sits in extensive parkland containing numerous walks and beautiful gardens, as well as an adventure playground for children. Gardens include an orangery, an Italian garden, and Dutch gardens.
Lyme Park (Pemberley exterior), Disley, Stockport, Cheshire , Tel: +44 (0)1663 762023, nationaltrust.org.uk
Originally a Tudor house, Lyme Park was altered to a stunning Italianate palace in the 18th century. Surrounded by a medieval deer park, the house features gardens that include a Victorian garden with a sunken parterre, an Edwardian rose garden, and flower borders in the style of Gertrude Jekyll.
The Old Rectory (Hunsford Parsonage), Teigh, Nr Oakham, Rutland, Tel: +44 (0)1572 787681 inquiries: torowen@btinternet.com
An attractive stone Georgian rectory with a spacious and well-tended garden, The Old Rectory is a B&B in the quiet village of Teigh, near Rutland Water. Next door is an unusual 18th-century church, which is open each day.

2007 MANSFIELD PARK
2007, starring Billie Piper and Blake Ritson

Newby Hall (Mansfield Park), Ripon, North Yorkshire, Tel: +44 (0)8454 504068, newbyhall.co.uk
Newby Hall is a splendid late 17th-century house, built under Sir Christopher Wren's guidance. Robert Adams later designed much of the interior, which has been beautifully restored. The house is set in 25 acres of award-winning gardens, featuring a species rose garden, an autumn garden, a white garden, a water garden, and even a tropical garden.

MANSFIELD PARK
1999, starring Frances O'Connor and Jonny Lee Miller

Kirby Hall (Mansfield Park), Corby, Northamptonshire, Tel: +44 (0)1536 203230, english-heritage.org.uk
One of the great Elizabethan houses, Kirby Hall was built to impress Elizabeth I, whose hoped-for visit never arrived. The magnificent gardens, laid out in a cutwork design, were added in the late 17th century, and were described at the time as "ye finest garden in England." They have been partly restored.

EMMA
1996, starring Kate Beckinsale and Mark Strong

Dorney Court (Randalls), Windsor, Berkshire, Tel: +44 (0)1628 604638 , dorneycourt.co.uk
Dorney Court, a picturesque gabled brick house, is a Grade 1 listed building. The house, beautifully restored, is set in more than a hundred acres of delightful gardens, woodland and farmland.

Sudeley Castle (Donwell Abbey exteriors), Winchcombe, Gloucestershire, Tel: +44 (0)1242 602308
sudeleycastle.co.uk

> A magnificent stone edifice set in the hills of the Cotswolds, Sudeley Castle dates to the 15th
> century and was once the home of King Henry VIII's only surviving wife, Katherine Parr.
> Among the many beautiful gardens, carefully restored, are a knot garden, a mulberry garden,
> a secret garden, a Victorian kitchen garden, and a garden in the old banqueting hall of the
> ruined portion of the castle.

EMMA
1996, starring Gwyneth Paltrow and Jeremy Northam

Claydon House, (Donwell Abbey/Crown ball scene), Middle Claydon, nr Buckingham,
Buckinghamshire , Tel: + 44 (0)1296 730349, nationaltrust.org.uk

> A fine example of a Georgian house, Claydon House is set in over 50 acres of parkland,
> including lakeside walks with beautiful views.

Mapperton (Randalls, and the garden behind Hartfield), Beaminster, Dorset,
Tel: +44 (0)1308 862645, mapperton.com

> Mapperton, originally an Elizabethan house, was enlarged in the late 17th century and remains
> mostly unchanged since that time. Voted "The Nation's Finest Manor House" in 2006 by
> Country Life, the handsome stone manor house is surrounded by terraced gardens including an
> Italianate garden with grottoes and a fountain court, 17th-century fish ponds and an orangery.

NORTHANGER ABBEY
1986, starring Katharine Schlesinger and Peter Firth

Corsham Court, (Fullerton rectory), Corsham, Wiltshire, Tel: +44 (0)1249 712214,
corsham-court.co.uk

> Corsham Court is a magnificent stone house dating in parts back to the 16th century. It sits
> amid a 350-acre landscape park extensively re-designed by Capability Brown in the 18th
> century, and later by Humphry Repton. The grounds include 17 acres of formal gardens and
> an extensive arboretum.

PERSUASION
2007, starring Sally Hawkins and Rupert Penry-Jones

Sheldon Manor (Uppercross), Chippenham, Wiltshire,
Tel: +44 (0)1249 653120, sheldonmanor.co.uk/

> Sheldon Manor is the oldest inhabited manor house in Wiltshire,
> with some sections dating back to the 13th century. The attractive
> gardens, which contain many old-fashioned roses and ancient
> yews, are currently being restored.

PERSUASION
1995, starring Amanda Root and Ciarán Hinds

Sheldon Manor (Uppercross), See entry under *Persuasion*, 1995.

Bibliography

Abercrombie, John. *The British Fruit-Gardener* . . . . London, 1779.

Abercrombie, John, and Thomas Mawe. *Every Man his Own Gardener* . . . . London, 1809.

Ambulator: *or A Pocket Companion in a Tour Round London* . . . . London, 1800.

Austen, Caroline. *My Aunt Jane Austen: A Memoir.* 1952. New ed. Winchester, 1991.

Austen, Jane. *Jane Austen's Letters.* 3rd ed. Deirdre Le Faye, ed. Oxford, 1997.

———. *Jane Austen: Collected Poems and Verse of the Austen family.* David Selwyn, ed. Manchester, 1996.

———. *The Novels of Jane Austen: The Text Based on Collation of the Early Editions.* R.W. Chapman, ed. 3rd ed. Oxford, 1932-34.

———. *Minor Works.* R.W. Chapman, ed., with revisions by B.C. Southam. Oxford, 1988.

Austen-Leigh, James Edward. *A Memoir of Jane Austen.* London, 1871.

Austen-Leigh, William and Richard, revised and enlarged by Deirdre Le Faye, *Jane Austen: A Family Record.* Boston, 1989.

Baker, James. *The Imperial Guide, with Picturesque Plans of the Great Post Roads* . . . . London, 1802.

Batey, Mavis. *Jane Austen and the English Landscape.* Chicago, 1996.

———. *Regency Gardens.* Princes Risborough, Buckinghamshire, U.K., 1995.

Blacker, Mary Rose. *Flora Domestica: A History of British Flower Arranging, 1500-1930.* London, 2000.

Blomfield, Reginald. *The Formal Garden in England.* London, 1901.

Brabourne, Edward, 1st Lord. *Letters of Jane Austen.* London, 1884.

Bradley, Richard. *New Improvements of Planting and Gardening* . . . . 7th ed. London, 1739.

Brayley, Edward W. *The Beauties of England and Wales; or Original Delineations . . . of Each County. Vol. VIII.* [Kent]. London, 1808.

Brayley, Edward W. and John Britton. *The Beauties of England and Wales* . . . . *Vol. VI* [Hampshire, Isle of Wight, Herefordshire]. London, 1805.

Britton, John, Joseph Nightingale, James Brewer, et al. *The Beauties of England and Wales . . . Wiltshire, Westmoreland, Warwickshire. Vol. XV.* London, 1814.

Buchoz, Pierre-Joseph. *The Toilet of Flora; Or, A Collection of the Most Simple and Approved Methods of Preparing Baths, Essences, Pomatums, Powders, Perfumes, and Sweet-Scented Waters, With Receipts for Cosmetics of every Kind* . . . . London, 1779.

Carpenter, T. Edward. *The Story of Jane Austen's Chawton Home.* Alton, Hampshire, n.d.

Collins, Irene. *Jane Austen: The Parson's Daughter.* London, 1998.

Combe, William. *The Tour of Doctor Syntax in Search of the Picturesque.* (1809) London, 1838.

Cottam, Graeme, Susie Grandfield, Sarah Parry, and Helen Scott. *Chawton House Library.* Whitefriars, Norwich, U.K., 2005.

Cowper, William. *Poems.* 5th ed. London, 1793.

Crease, James. *Hints for the Preservation of Wood-Work Exposed to the Weather.* London, 1808.

Crossley, Alan, ed. "Blenheim: Blenheim Palace." In *A History of the County of Oxford: Volume 12: Wootton Hundred (South) including Woodstock.* 1990. Accessed at british-history.ac.uk/report. asp?compid=7897.

Daniels, Stephen. *Humphry Repton: Landscape Gardening and the Geography of Georgian England.* New Haven, 1999.

Driver, Abraham and William Driver. *General View of the Agriculture in the County of Hants, with Observations on the Means of its Improvement.* London, 1794.

Duckworth, Alistair M. *The Improvement of the Estate: A Study of Jane Austen's Novels.* 1971. Reprint, Baltimore, 1994.

Edwards, Anne-Marie. *In the Steps of Jane Austen.* 1991. New ed., Madison, Wisconsin, 2003.

Ellis, Thomas. *The Gardener's Pocket-Calendar: Containing the Most Approved Methods of Cultivating the Useful and Ornamental Plants . . . .* London, 1776.

Fawcett, Trevor. *Bath Administer'd: Corporation Affairs at the 18th-Century Spa.* Bath, 2001.

Fearnley-Whittingstall, Jane. *The Garden: An English Love Affair. One Thousand Years of Gardening.* 2002. Reprint, London, 2003.

Fleming, Laurence and Alan Gore. *The English Garden.* London, 1979.

Freeman, Jean. *Jane Austen in Bath.* 1969. Reprint, Alton, Hampshire, 1974.

Foster, Paul and David Standing. *Landscape and Labour: Gilbert White's Garden (1751-93).* Selborne, Hampshire, U.K., 2005.

Gilpin, William. *Observations on the Western Parts of England, Relative Chiefly to Picturesque Beauty* . . . . London, 1798.

Girouard, Mark. *Life in the English Country House.* New Haven, 1978.

Goede, Christian A.G. *The Stranger in England; or, Travels in Great Britain* . . . . London, 1807.

Grimshaw, John. *The Gardener's Atlas: The Origins, Discovery, and Cultivation of the World's Most Popular Garden Plants.* Buffalo, N.Y., 2002.

Henshaw, Henry. *Hampshire: Historical Notes and Anecdotes.* Steventon, Hampshire, U.K., 1997.

Hill, Constance. *Jane Austen, Her Homes and Her Friends.* London, 1901.

Home, Henry. *Elements of Criticism.* Edinburgh, 1762.

Honan, Park. *Jane Austen: Her Life.* New York, 1989.

Hughson, David. *London; Being an Accurate History and Description of the British Metropolis and Its Neighborhood* . . . . London, 1807.

———. *Walks through London* . . . . London, 1817.

Hunt, John Dixon and Peter Willis, eds. *The Genius of the Place: The English Landscape Garden 1620-1820.* 1975. New ed., Cambridge, Massachusetts, 1988.

Jane's Hand: The Jane Austen Songbooks. Mary Jane Newman, artistic director. Vox 7537.

Jerrold, Walter. *Highways and Byways in Kent.* London, 1907.

Jones, Mike. *An Introduction to the Royal Pavilion's Garden.* Brighton, n.d.

Joseph Spence Papers. James Marshall and Marie-Louise Osborn Collection, Beinecke Rare Book and Manuscript Library. Accessed at webtext.library.yale.edu/xml2html/beinecke. spence.con.html#SV

The Juvenile Gardener, Written by a Lady for the Use of Her Own Children . . . . London, 1824.

Kent, Elizabeth. *Flora Domestica, Or The Portable Flower-Garden.* London, 1823.

"Knight's Landscape, A Didactic Poem." In *The Monthly Review; Or Literary Journal, Enlarged.* May to August. London, 1794.

Lady of Distinction. *The Mirror of the Graces.* London, 1811. Facsimile printed as *Regency Etiquette: The Mirror of Graces (1811),* 1997.

Laird, Mark. *The Flowering of the Landscape Garden: English Pleasure Grounds 1720-1800.* Philadelphia, 1999.

Lane, Maggie. *A Charming Place: Bath in the Life and Novels of Jane Austen.* 1988. Reprint, Bath, 2000.

Le Faye, Deirdre. *A Chronology of Jane Austen and her Family.* Cambridge, U.K., 2006.

———. *Fanny Knight's Diaries: Jane Austen Through Her Niece's Eyes.* Winchester, 2000.

Leigh, Samuel, *Leigh's New Picture of England and Wales . . . .* London, 1820.

"Letter from a young gentleman on his travels to his friends in America." In Joseph Dennie, ed., *The Port Folio. Vol. III.* Philadelphia and New York, 1809.

The London General Gazetteer, Or Geographical Dictionary . . . . London, 1825.

Longstaffe-Gowan, Todd. *The London Town Garden.* New Haven, 2001.

Loudon, John C. *An Encyclopaedia of Gardening; Comprising the Theory and Practice of Horticulture, Floriculture, Arboriculture, and Landscape-Gardening . . . .* London, 1822.

———. *Hints on the Formation of Gardens and Pleasure Grounds . . . .* London, 1813.

———. *Observations on the Formation and Management of Useful and Ornamental Plantations; On the Theory and Practice of Landscape Gardening . . . .* Edinburgh, 1804.

Luckombe, Philip. *The Beauties of England . . . .* 2nd ed. London, 1764.

Marshall, William. *On Planting and Rural Ornament. A Practical Treatise.* 3rd ed. London, 1803.

———. *Planting and Ornamental Gardening; A Practical Treatise.* London, 1785.

Marshall, William Humphrey. *A Review of the Reports to the Board of Agriculture; from the Western Department of England . . . .* London, 1810.

Mavor, William. *New Description of Blenheim, the Seat of His Grace the Duke of Marlborough: Containing . . . a Picturesque Tour of the Gardens and Parks . . . .* 6th ed. Oxford, 1803.

Maxwell, Roy. "Beneath the Surface: Channel Four's Time Team comes to Bath." In *Royal Crescent Society Newsletter,* no. 50. Bath, 2003. Accessed at royalcrescentbath.com/History.htm

McPhail, James. *The Gardener's Remembrancer: Throughout the Year, Exhibiting the Newest and Most Improved Methods of Manuring, Digging, Sowing, Planting, Pruning, and Training . . . .* London, 1807.

Miller, Philip. *The Gardeners Kalendar; Directing what Works are necessary to be performed Every Month in the Kitchen, Fruit, and Pleasure Gardens . . . .* 15th ed. London, 1769.

"Miss Austen." In *Hampshire Notes and Queries,* Reprinted from the *Winchester Observer & County News.* Vol. I. Winchester, 1883.

Moncrieff, William Thomas. *The Visitor's New Guide to the Spa of Leamington Priors, And its Vicinity: Including . . . Stonleigh* [sic] *Abbey; . . . .* Leamington, 1818.

Neale, John P. *Views of the Seats of Noblemen and Gentlemen, in England, Wales, Scotland, and Ireland. Second Series. Vol. III.* London, 1826.

The New Bath Guide; Or, Useful Pocket Companion, for all Persons residing at or resorting to this Ancient City . . . . Bath, 1799.

Nicolson, Nigel. *Godmersham Park, Kent, before, during, and since Jane Austen's day.* Alton, Hampshire, U.K., 1996.

———. *The World of Jane Austen.* London, 1991.

O'Keeffe, John. *The London Hermit.* In *The Dramatic Works of John O'Keeffe, Esq.* London, 1798.

Phillips, Henry. *Sylva Florifera: The Shrubbery, Historically and Botanically Treated; With Observations on the Formation of Ornamental Plantations and Picturesque Scenery.* London, 1823.

Porter, Anna Maria. *Ballad Romances and Other Poems.* Philadelphia, 1816.

Porter, Roy. *London: A Social History.* Cambridge, Massachusetts, 1994.

Price, Uvedale. *Essays on the Picturesque, As Compared with the Sublime and the Beautiful; and, On the Use of Studying Pictures, For the Purpose of Improving Real Landscape.* London, 1810.

"Private Masquerade." In *The Sporting Magazine.* [June] Vol. XVI. London, 1800.

"The Proceedings of the Old Bailey London 1674 to 1834" (garden theft cases). Online at oldbaileyonline.org/

Quest-Ritson, Charles. *The English Garden: A Social History.* Boston, 2003.

Repton, Humphry. *The Landscape Gardening and Landscape Architecture of the Late Humphry Repton, Esq., Being His Entire Works on Their Subjects.* John Loudon, ed. Edinburgh, 1840.

Rudge, Thomas. *General View of the Agriculture of the County of Gloucester. Drawn Up for the Consideration of the Board of Agriculture and Internal Improvement.* London, 1807.

Rundell, Maria. *A New System of Domestic Cookery.* London, 1808.

Sheppard, F.H.W., ed. "Henrietta Street and Maiden Lane Area: Henrietta Street." In *Survey of London. Vol. 36: Covent Garden.* 1970. Accessed at british_history.ac.uk/report. asp?compid=46126.

Silliman, Benjamin. *A Journal of Travels in England, Holland and Scotland, and of Two Passages Over the Atlantic in the Years 1805 and 1806 . . . .* 3rd ed. New Haven, 1820.

Simond, Louis. *Journal of a Tour and Residence in Great Britain During the Years 1810 and 1811.* Edinburgh, 1815.

Smith, David Waldron. *Jane Austen in Kent.* Westerham, Kent, U.K., 1981.

Smith, James Edward. *English Botany or Coloured Figures of British Plants . . . .* London, 1803.

Society of Practical Gardeners. *Rural Recreations; or the Gardener's Instructor . . . .* London, 1802.

Spiker, Samuel H. *Travels through England, Wales, & Scotland, in the Year 1816.* London, 1820.

Thorold, Peter. *The London Rich: The Creation of a Great City, from 1666 to the Present.* London, 1999.

Timbs, John. *A Picturesque Promenade Round Dorking, In Surrey.* London, 1822.

Tomalin, Claire. *Jane Austen: A Life.* New York, 1998.

"Town Gardens." In *Gentleman's Magazine: And Historical Chronicle.* Vol. 61, part 2. 1791.

Tuer, Andrew W. *Old London Street Cries and the Cries of To-Day . . . .* London, 1885.

Vancouver, Charles. *General View of the Agriculture of Hampshire, Including the Isle of Wight. Drawn up for the Board of Agriculture and Internal Improvement.* London, 1810.

Wallis, John. *London: Being a Complete Guide to the British Capital.* 4th ed. London, 1814.

Warner, Richard. *Bath Characters or Sketches from Life.* London, 1808.

———. *A New Guide through Bath, and its Environs.* Bath and London, 1811.

Watson, Winifred. *Jane Austen in London.* Alton, Hampshire, 1960.

Whately, Thomas. *Observations on Modern Gardening, and Laying Out Pleasure-Grounds, Parks, Farms, Ridings . . . .* London, 1801.

Wilson, Margaret. *Almost Another Sister: The Story of Fanny Knight, Jane Austen's Favourite Niece.* Maidstone, Kent, U.K., 1998.

Index